THE CASE AGAINST THE FED

The Ludwig von Mises Institute
acknowledges with gratitude the
generosity of
Mr. Doug Casey and the
Eugene B. Casey Foundation and the
Hon. Ron Paul and CTAF, Inc.,
who made the original publication
of this book possible.

THE CASE
AGAINST THE FED

MURRAY N. ROTHBARD

Ludwig
von Mises
Institute

AUBURN, ALABAMA

Copyright © 1994 by Murray N. Rothbard
Copyright © 2007 by the Ludwig von Mises Institute

Ludwig von Mises Institute, 518 West Magnolia Avenue, Auburn, Ala. 36832; www.mises.org

ISBN: 978-0-945466-17-8

Cover photo by David Hittle

Contents

Introduction:
Money and Politics

By far the most secret and least accountable operation of the federal government is not, as one might expect, the CIA, DIA, or some other super-secret intelligence agency. The CIA and other intelligence operations are under control of the Congress. They are accountable: a Congressional committee supervises these operations, controls their budgets, and is informed of their covert activities. It is true that the committee hearings and activities are closed to the public; but at least the people's representatives in Congress insure some accountability for these secret agencies.

It is little known, however, that there is a federal agency that tops the others in secrecy by a country mile. The Federal Reserve System is accountable to no one; it has no budget; it is subject to no audit; and no Congressional committee knows of, or can truly supervise, its operations. The Federal Reserve, virtually in total control of the nation's vital monetary system, is accountable to nobody—and this strange situation, if acknowledged at all, is invariably trumpeted as a virtue.

Thus, when the first Democratic president in over a decade was inaugurated in 1993, the maverick and venerable Democratic Chairman of the House Banking Committee, Texan Henry B. Gonzalez, optimistically introduced some of his favorite projects for opening up the Fed to public scrutiny. His proposals seemed mild; he did not call for full-fledged Congressional control of the Fed's budget. The Gonzalez bill required full independent audits of the Fed's operations; videotaping the meetings of the Fed's policy-making committee; and releasing detailed minutes of the policy meetings within a week, rather than the Fed being allowed, as it is now, to issue vague summaries of its decisions six weeks later. In addition, the presidents of the twelve regional Federal Reserve Banks would be chosen by the president of the United States rather than, as they are now, by the commercial banks of the respective regions.

It was to be expected that Fed Chairman Alan Greenspan would strongly resist any such proposals. After all, it is in the nature of bureaucrats to resist any encroachment on their unbridled power. Seemingly more surprising was the rejection of the Gonzalez plan by President Clinton, whose power, after all, would be enhanced by the measure. The Gonzalez reforms, the President declared, "run the risk of undermining market confidence in the Fed."

On the face of it, this presidential reaction, though traditional among chief executives, is rather puzzling. After all, doesn't a democracy depend upon the right of the people to know what is going on in the government for which they must vote? Wouldn't knowledge and full disclosure strengthen the faith of the American public in their monetary authorities? Why should public knowledge "undermine market confidence"? Why does "market confidence" depend on assuring far less public scrutiny than is accorded keepers of military secrets that might benefit foreign enemies? What is going on here?

The standard reply of the Fed and its partisans is that any such measures, however marginal, would encroach on the Fed's "independence from politics," which is invoked as a kind of self-evident absolute. The monetary system is highly important, it is claimed, and therefore the Fed must enjoy absolute independence.

"Independent of politics" has a nice, neat ring to it, and has been a staple of proposals for bureaucratic intervention and power ever since the Progressive Era. Sweeping the streets; control of seaports; regulation of industry; providing social security; these and many other functions of government are held to be "too important" to be subject to the vagaries of political whims. But it is one thing to say that private, or market, activities should be free of government control, and "independent of politics" in that sense. But these are *government* agencies and operations we are talking about, and to say that *government* should be "independent of politics" conveys very different implications. For government, unlike private industry on the market, is not accountable either to stockholders or consumers. Government can only be accountable to the public and to its representatives in the legislature; and if government becomes "independent of politics" it can only mean that that sphere of government becomes an absolute self-perpetuating oligarchy, accountable to no one and never subject to the public's ability to change its personnel or to "throw the rascals out." If no person or group, whether stockholders or voters, can displace a ruling elite, then such an elite becomes more suitable for a dictatorship than for an allegedly democratic country. And yet it is curious how many self-proclaimed champions of "democracy," whether domestic or global, rush to defend the alleged ideal of the total independence of the Federal Reserve.

Representative Barney Frank (D., Mass.), a co-sponsor of the Gonzalez bill, points out that "if you take the principles that people are talking about nowadays," such as "reforming government and opening up government—the Fed violates it more than any other branch of government." On what basis, then, should the vaunted "principle" of an independent Fed be maintained?

It is instructive to examine who the defenders of this alleged principle may be, and the tactics they are using. Presumably one political agency the Fed particularly wants to be independent from is the U.S. Treasury. And yet Frank Newman, President Clinton's Under Secretary of the Treasury for Domestic Finance, in rejecting the Gonzalez reform, states: "The Fed is independent and that's one of the underlying concepts." In addition, a revealing little point is made by the *New York Times*, in noting the Fed's reaction to the Gonzalez bill: "The Fed is already working behind the scenes to organize battalions of bankers to howl about efforts to politicize the central bank" (*New York Times*, October 12, 1993). True enough. But why should these "battalions of bankers" be so eager and willing to mobilize in behalf of the Fed's absolute control of the monetary and banking system? Why should bankers be so ready to defend a federal agency which controls and regulates them, and virtually determines the operations of the banking system? Shouldn't private banks want to have some sort of check, some curb, upon their lord and master? Why should a regulated and controlled industry be so much in love with the unchecked power of their own federal controller?

Let us consider any other private industry. Wouldn't it be just a tad suspicious if, say, the insurance industry demanded unchecked power for their state regulators, or the trucking industry total power for the ICC, or the drug companies were clamoring for total and secret power to the Food and Drug Administration? So shouldn't we be very suspicious of the oddly cozy relationship between the banks and the Federal Reserve? What's going on here? Our task in this volume is to open up the Fed to the scrutiny it is unfortunately not getting in the public arena.

Absolute power and lack of accountability by the Fed are generally defended on one ground alone: that any change would weaken the Federal Reserve's allegedly inflexible commitment to wage a seemingly permanent "fight against inflation." This is the Johnny-one-note of the Fed's defense of its unbridled power. The Gonzalez reforms, Fed officials warn, might be seen by financial markets "as weakening the Fed's ability to fight inflation" (*New York Times*, October 8, 1993). In subsequent Congressional testimony, Chairman Alan Greenspan elaborated this point. Politicians, and presumably the public, are eternally tempted to expand the money supply and thereby aggravate (price) inflation. Thus to Greenspan:

> The temptation is to step on the monetary accelerator or at least to avoid the monetary brake until after the next election. . . . Giving in to such temptations is likely to impart an inflationary bias to the economy and could lead to instability, recession, and economic stagnation.

The Fed's lack of accountability, Greenspan added, is a small price to pay to avoid "putting the conduct of monetary policy under the close influence of politicians subject to short-term election cycle pressure" (*New York Times*, October 14, 1993).

So there we have it. The public, in the mythology of the Fed and its supporters, is a great beast, continually subject to a lust for inflating the money supply and therefore for subjecting the economy to inflation and its dire consequences. Those dreaded all-too-frequent inconveniences called "elections" subject politicians to these temptations, especially in political institutions such as the House of Representatives who come before the public every two years and are therefore particularly responsive to the public will. The Federal Reserve, on the other hand, guided by monetary experts independent of the public's lust for inflation, stands ready at all times to promote the long-run public interest by manning the battlements in an eternal fight against the Gorgon of inflation. The public, in short, is in desperate need of absolute control of money by the Federal Reserve to save it from itself and its short-term lusts and temptations. One monetary economist, who spent much of the 1920s and 1930s setting up Central Banks throughout the Third World, was commonly referred to as "the money doctor." In our current therapeutic age, perhaps Greenspan and his confrères would like to be considered as monetary "therapists," kindly but stern taskmasters whom we invest with total power to save us from ourselves.

But in this administering of therapy, where do the private bankers fit in? Very neatly, according to Federal Reserve officials. The Gonzalez proposal to have the president instead of regional bankers appoint regional Fed presidents would, in the eyes of those officials, "make it harder for the Fed to clamp down on inflation." Why? Because, the "sure way" to "minimize inflation" is "to have private bankers appoint the regional bank presidents." And why is this private banker role such a "sure way"? Because, according to the Fed officials, private bankers "are among the world's fiercest inflation hawks" (*New York Times*, October 12, 1993).

The worldview of the Federal Reserve and its advocates is now complete. Not only are the public and politicians responsive to it eternally subject to the temptation to inflate; but it is important for the Fed to have a cozy partnership with private bankers. Private bankers, as "the world's fiercest inflation hawks," can only bolster the Fed's eternal devotion to battling against inflation.

There we have the ideology of the Fed as reflected in its own propaganda, as well as respected Establishment transmission belts such as the *New York Times*, and in pronouncements and textbooks by countless economists. Even those economists who would like to see more inflation accept and repeat the Fed's image of its own role. And yet every aspect of this mythology is the very reverse of the truth. We cannot think straight about money, banking, or the Federal Reserve until this fraudulent legend has been exposed and demolished.

There is, however, one and only one aspect of the common legend that is indeed correct: that the overwhelmingly dominant cause of the virus of chronic price inflation is inflation, or expansion, of the supply of money. Just as an increase in the production or supply of cotton will cause that crop to be cheaper on the market; so will the creation of more money make its unit of money, each franc or dollar, cheaper and worth less in purchasing power of goods on the market.

But let us consider this agreed-upon fact in the light of the above myth about the Federal Reserve. We supposedly have the public clamoring for inflation while the Federal Reserve, flanked by its allies the nation's bankers, resolutely sets its face against this short-sighted public clamor. But how is the public supposed to go about achieving this inflation? How can the public create, i.e., "print," more money? It would be difficult to do so, since only one institution in the society is legally allowed to print money. Anyone who tries to print money is engaged in the high crime of "counterfeiting," which the federal government takes very seriously indeed. Whereas the government may take a benign view of all other torts and crimes, including mugging, robbery, and murder, and it may worry about the "deprived youth" of the criminal and treat him tenderly, there is *one* group of criminals whom no government ever coddles: the counterfeiters. The counterfeiter is hunted down seriously and efficiently, and he is salted away for a very long time; for he is committing a crime that the government takes very seriously: he is interfering with the government's revenue: specifically, the monopoly power to print money enjoyed by the Federal Reserve.

"Money," in our economy, is pieces of paper issued by the Federal Reserve, on which are engraved the following: "This Note is Legal Tender for all Debts, Private, and Public."

This "Federal Reserve Note," and nothing else, is money, and all vendors and creditors must accept these notes, like it or not.

So: if the chronic inflation undergone by Americans, and in almost every other country, is caused by the continuing creation of new money, *and if* in each country its governmental "Central Bank" (in the United States, the Federal Reserve) is the sole monopoly source and creator of all money, *who then* is responsible for the blight of inflation? Who except the very institution that is solely empowered to create money, that is, the Fed (and the Bank of England, and the Bank of Italy, and other central banks) *itself?*

In short: even before examining the problem in detail, we should already get a glimmer of the truth: that the drum-fire of propaganda that the Fed is manning the ramparts against the menace of inflation brought about by others is nothing less than a deceptive shell game. The culprit solely responsible for inflation, the Federal Reserve, is continually engaged in raising a hue-and-cry about "inflation," for which virtually *everyone else* in society seems to be responsible. What we are seeing is the old ploy by the robber who starts shouting "Stop, thief!" and runs down the street pointing ahead at others. We begin to see why it has always been important for the Fed, and for other Central Banks, to invest themselves with an aura of solemnity and mystery. For, as we shall see more fully, if the public knew what was going on, if it was able to rip open the curtain covering the inscrutable Wizard of Oz, it would soon discover that the Fed, far from being the indispensable solution to the problem of inflation, is itself the heart and cause of the problem. What

we need is not a totally independent, all-powerful Fed; what
we need is no Fed at all.

The Genesis of Money

It is impossible to understand money and how it functions,
and therefore how the Fed functions, without looking at the
logic of how money, banking, and Central Banking developed. The reason is that money is unique in possessing a vital
historical component. You can explain the needs and the
demand for everything else: for bread, computers, concerts,
airplanes, medical care, etc., solely by how these goods and
services are valued now by consumers. For all of these goods
are valued and purchased for their own sake. But "money,"
dollars, francs, lira, etc., is purchased and accepted in exchange not for any value the paper tickets have *per se* but
because everyone expects that everyone else will accept
these tickets in exchange. And these expectations are perva-
sive because these tickets have indeed been accepted in the
immediate and more remote past. An analysis of the history
of money, then, is indispensable for insight into how the
monetary system works today.

Money did not and never could begin by some arbitrary
social contract, or by some government agency decreeing
that everyone has to accept the tickets it issues. Even coercion
could not force people and institutions to accept meaningless
tickets that they had not heard of or that bore no relation to
any other pre-existing money. Money arises on the free
market, as individuals on the market try to facilitate the
vital process of exchange. The market is a network, a
lattice-work of two people or institutions exchanging two

different commodities. Individuals specialize in producing different goods or services, and then exchanging these goods on terms they agree upon. Jones produces a barrel of fish and exchanges it for Smith's bushel of wheat. Both parties make the exchange because they expect to benefit; and so the free market consists of a network of exchanges that are mutually beneficial at every step of the way.

But this system of "direct exchange" of useful goods, or "barter," has severe limitations which exchangers soon run up against. Suppose that Smith dislikes fish, but Jones, a fisherman, would like to buy his wheat. Jones then tries to find a product, say butter, not for his own use but in order to resell to Smith. Jones is here engaging in "indirect exchange," where he purchases butter, not for its own sake, but for use as a "medium," or middle-term, in the exchange. In other cases, goods are "indivisible" and cannot be chopped up into small parts to be used in direct exchange. Suppose, for example, that Robbins would like to sell a tractor, and then purchase a myriad of different goods: horses, wheat, rope, barrels, etc. Clearly, he can't chop the tractor into seven or eight parts, and exchange each part for a good he desires. What he will have to do is to engage in "indirect exchange," that is, to sell the tractor for a more divisible commodity, say 100 pounds of butter, and then slice the butter into divisible parts and exchange each part for the good he desires. Robbins, again, would then be using butter as a medium of exchange.

Once any particular commodity starts to be used as a medium, this very process has a spiralling, or snowballing, effect. If, for example, several people in a society begin to use butter as a medium, people will realize that in that particular region butter is becoming especially marketable, or acceptable in exchange, and so they will demand more butter in exchange for use as a medium. And so, as its use as a medium becomes more widely known, this use feeds upon itself, until rapidly the commodity comes into general employment in the society as a medium of exchange. A commodity that is in general use as a medium is defined as a *money*.

Once a good comes into use as a money, the market expands rapidly, and the economy becomes remarkably more productive and prosperous. The reason is that the price system becomes enormously simplified. A "price" is simply the terms of exchange, the ratio of the quantities of the two goods being traded. In every exchange, x amount of one commodity is exchanged for y amount of another. Take the Smith-Jones trade noted above. Suppose that Jones exchanges 2 barrels of fish for Smith's 1 bushel of wheat. In that case, the "price" of wheat in terms of fish is 2 barrels of fish per bushel. Conversely, the "price" of fish in terms of wheat is one-half a bushel per barrel. In a system of barter, knowing the relative price of anything would quickly become impossibly complicated: thus, the price of a hat might be 10 candy bars, or 6 loaves of bread, or 1/10 of a TV set, and on and on. But once a money is established on the market, then every single exchange includes the money-commodity as one of its two commodities. Jones will sell fish for the money commodity, and will then "sell" the money in exchange for wheat, shoes, tractors, entertainment, or whatever. And Smith will sell his wheat in the same manner. As a result, every price will be reckoned simply in terms of its "money-price," its price in terms of the common money-commodity.

Thus, suppose that butter has become the society's money by this market process. In that case, all prices of goods or services are reckoned in their respective money-prices; thus, a hat might exchange for 15 ounces of butter, a candy bar may be priced at 1.5 ounces of butter, a TV set at 150 ounces of butter, etc. If you want to know how the market price of a hat compares to other goods, you don't have to figure each relative price directly; all you have to know is that the money-price of a hat is 15 ounces of butter, or 1 ounce of gold, or whatever the money-commodity is, and then it will be easy to reckon the various goods in terms of their respective money-prices.

Another grave problem with a world of barter is that it is impossible for any business firm to calculate how it's doing, whether it is making profits or incurring losses, beyond a very primitive estimate. Suppose that you are a business firm, and you are trying to calculate your income, and your expenses, for the previous month. And you list your income: "let's see, last month we took in 20 yards of string, 3 codfish, 4 cords of lumber, 3 bushels of wheat . . . etc.," and "we paid out: 5 empty barrels, 8 pounds of cotton, 30 bricks, 5 pounds of beef." How in the world could you figure out how well you are doing? Once a money is established in an economy, however, business calculation becomes easy: "Last month, we took in 500 ounces of gold, and paid out 450 ounces of gold. Net profit, 50 gold ounces." The development of a general medium of exchange, then, is a crucial requisite to the development of any sort of flourishing market economy.

In the history of mankind, every society, including primitive tribes, rapidly developed money in the above manner, on the market. Many commodities have been used as money: iron hoes in Africa, salt in West Africa, sugar in the Caribbean, beaver skins in Canada, codfish in colonial New England, tobacco in colonial Maryland and Virginia. In German prisoner-of-war camps of British soldiers during World War II, the continuing trading of CARE packages soon resulted in a "money" in which all other goods were priced and reckoned. Cigarettes became the money in these camps, not because of any imposition by German or British officers or from any sudden agreement: it emerged "organically" from barter trading in spontaneously developed markets within the camps.

Throughout all these eras and societies, however, two commodities, if the society had access to them, were easily able to outcompete the rest, and to establish themselves on the market as the only moneys. These were gold and silver.

Why gold and silver? (And to a lesser extent, copper, when the other two were unavailable.) Because gold and silver are superior in various "moneyish" qualities—qualities that a good needs to have to be selected by the market as money. Gold and silver were highly valuable in themselves, for their beauty; their supply was limited enough to have a roughly stable value, but not so scarce that they could not readily be parcelled out for use (platinum would fit into the latter category); they were in wide demand, and were easily portable; they were highly divisible, as they could be sliced into small pieces and keep a *pro rata* share of their value; they could be easily made homogeneous, so that one ounce would look like another; and they were highly durable, thus preserving a store of value into the indefinite future. (Mixed with a small amount of alloy, gold coins have literally been able to last for thousands of years.) Outside the hermetic prisoner-of-war camp environment, cigarettes would have done badly as money because they are too easily manufactured; in the outside world, the supply of cigarettes would have multiplied rapidly and its value diminished nearly to zero. (Another problem of cigarettes as money is their lack of durability.)

Every good on the market exchanges in terms of relevant quantitative units: we trade in "bushels" of wheat; "packs" of 20 cigarettes; "a pair" of shoelaces; one TV set; etc. These units boil down to number, weight, or volume. Metals invariably trade and therefore are priced in terms of *weight*: tons, pounds, ounces, etc. And so moneys have generally been traded in units of weight, in whatever language used in that society. Accordingly, every modern currency unit originated as a *unit of weight of gold or silver*. Why is the British currency unit called "the pound sterling?" Because originally, in the Middle Ages, that's precisely what it was: a pound weight of silver. The "dollar" began in sixteenth-century Bohemia, as a well-liked and widely circulated one-ounce silver coin minted by the Count of Schlick, who lived in Joachimsthal. They became known as Joachimsthalers, or Schlichtenthalers, and human nature being what it is, they were soon popularly abbreviated as "thalers," later to become "dollars" in Spain. When the United States was founded, we shifted from the British pound currency to the dollar, defining the dollar as approximately 1/20 of a gold ounce, or 0.8 silver ounces.

What Is the Optimum Quantity of Money?

The total stock, or "supply," or quantity of money in any area or society at any given time is simply the sum total of all the ounces of gold, or units of money, in that particular society or region. Economists have often been concerned with the question: what is the "optimal" quantity of money, what should the total money stock be, at the present time? How fast should that total "grow"?

If we consider this common question carefully, however, it should strike us as rather peculiar. How come, after all, that no one addresses the question: what is the "optimal supply" of canned peaches today or in the future? Or Nintendo games? Or ladies' shoes? In fact, the very question is absurd. A crucial fact in any economy is that all resources are scarce in relation to human wants; if a good were not scarce, it would be superabundant, and therefore be priced, like air, at zero on the market. Therefore, other things being equal, the more goods available to us the better. If someone finds a new copper field, or discovers a better way of producing wheat or steel, these increases in supply of goods confer a social benefit. The more goods the better, unless we returned to the Garden of Eden; for this would mean that more natural scarcity has been alleviated, and living standards in society have increased. It is because people sense the absurdity of such a question that it is virtually never raised.

But why, then, does an optimal supply of money even arise as a problem? Because while money, as we have seen, is indispensable to the functioning of any economy beyond the most primitive level, and while the existence of money confers enormous social benefits, this by no means implies, as in the case of all other goods, that, other things being equal, the more the better. For when the supplies of other goods increase, we either have more consumer goods that can be used, or more resources or capital that can be used up in producing a greater supply of consumer goods. But of what direct benefit is an increase in the supply of money?

Money, after all, can neither be eaten nor used up in production. The money-commodity, functioning as money, can only be used in exchange, in facilitating the transfer of goods and services, and in making economic calculation possible. But once a money has been established in the market, no increases in its supply are needed, and they perform no genuine social function. As we know from general economic theory, the invariable result of an increase in the supply of a good is to lower its price. For all products except money, such an increase is socially beneficial, since it means that production and living standards have increased in response to consumer demand. If steel or bread or houses are more plentiful and cheaper than before, everyone's standard of living benefits. But an increase in the supply of money cannot relieve the natural scarcity of consumer or capital goods; all it does is to make the dollar or the franc cheaper, that is, lower its purchasing power in terms of all other goods and services. Once a good has been established as money on the market, then, it exerts its full power as a mechanism of exchange or an instrument of calculation. All that an increase in the quantity of dollars can do is to dilute the effectiveness, the purchasing-power, of each dollar. Hence, the great truth of monetary theory emerges: once a commodity is in sufficient supply to be adopted as a money, no further increase in the supply of money is needed. *Any* quantity of money in society is "optimal." Once a money is established, an increase in its supply confers no social benefit.

Does that mean that, once gold became money, all mining and production of gold was a waste? No, because a greater supply of gold allowed an increase in gold's *non-*monetary use: more abundant and lower-priced jewelry, ornaments, fillings for teeth, etc. But more gold *as money* was not needed in the economy. Money, then, is unique among goods and services since increases in its supply are neither beneficial nor needed; indeed, such increases only dilute money's unique value: to be a worthy object of exchange.

Monetary Inflation and Counterfeiting

Suppose that a precious metal such as gold becomes a society's money, and a certain weight of gold becomes the currency unit in which all prices and assets are reckoned. Then, so long as the society remains on this pure gold or silver "standard," there will probably be only gradual annual increases in the supply of money, from the output of gold mines. The supply of gold is severely limited, and it is costly to mine further gold; and the great durability of gold means that any annual output will constitute a small portion of the total gold stock accumulated over the centuries. The currency will remain of roughly stable value; in a progressing economy, the increased annual production of goods will more than offset the gradual increase in the money stock. The result will be a gradual fall in the price level, an increase in the purchasing power of the currency unit or gold ounce, year after year. The gently falling price level will mean a steady annual rise in the purchasing power of the dollar or franc, encouraging the saving of money and investment in future production. A rising output and falling price level signifies a steady increase in the standard of living for each person in society. Typically, the cost of living falls steadily, while money wage rates remain the same, meaning that "real" wage rates, or the living standards of every worker, increase steadily year by year. We are now so conditioned by permanent price inflation that the idea of prices *falling* every year is difficult to grasp. And yet, prices generally fell every year from the beginning of the Industrial Revolution in the latter part of the eighteenth century until 1940, with the exception of periods of major war, when the governments inflated the money supply radically and drove up prices, after which they would gradually fall once more. We have to realize that falling prices did not mean depression, since costs were falling due to increased productivity, so that profits were not sinking. If we look at the spectacular drop in prices (in *real* even more than in money terms) in recent years in such particularly booming fields as computers, calculators, and TV sets, we can see that falling prices by no means have to connote depression.

But let us suppose that in this idyll of prosperity, sound money, and successful monetary calculation, a serpent appears in Eden: the temptation to *counterfeit*, to fashion a near-valueless object so that it would fool people into thinking it was the money-commodity. It is instructive to trace the result. Counterfeiting creates a problem to the extent that it is "successful," i.e., to the extent that the counterfeit is so well crafted that it is not found out.

Suppose that Joe Doakes and his merry men have invented a perfect counterfeit: under a gold standard, a brass or plastic object that would look exactly like a gold coin, or, in the present paper money standard, a $10 bill that exactly simulates a $10 Federal Reserve Note. What would happen?

In the first place, the aggregate money supply of the country would increase by the amount counterfeited; equally important, the new money will appear *first* in the hands of the counterfeiters themselves. Counterfeiting, in short, involves a twofold process: (1) increasing the total supply of money, thereby driving up the prices of goods and services and driving down the purchasing power of the money-unit; and (2) changing the distribution of income and wealth, by putting disproportionately more money into the hands of the counterfeiters.

The first part of the process, increasing the total money supply in the country, was the focus of the "quantity theory" of the British classical economists from David Hume to Ricardo, and continues to be the focus of Milton Friedman and the monetarist "Chicago school." David Hume, in order to demonstrate the inflationary and non-productive effect of paper money, in effect postulated what I like to call the "Angel Gabriel" model, in which the Angel, after hearing pleas for more money, magically doubled each person's stock of money overnight. (In this case, the Angel Gabriel would be the "counterfeiter," albeit for benevolent motives.) It is clear that while everyone would be euphoric from their seeming doubling of monetary wealth, society would in no way be better off: for there would be no increase in capital or productivity or supply of goods. As people rushed out and spent the new money, the only impact would be an approximate doubling of all prices, and the purchasing power of the dollar or franc would be cut in half, with no social benefit being conferred. An increase of money can only dilute the effectiveness of each unit of money. Milton Friedman's more modern though equally magical version is that of his "helicopter effect," in which he postulates that the annual increase of money created by the Federal Reserve is showered on each person proportionately to his current money stock by magical governmental helicopters.

While Hume's analysis is perceptive and correct so far as it goes, it leaves out the vital redistributive effect. Friedman's "helicopter effect" seriously distorts the analysis by being so constructed that redistributive effects are ruled out from the very beginning. The point is that while we can assume benign motives for the Angel Gabriel, we cannot make the same assumption for the counterfeiting government or the Federal Reserve. Indeed, for any earthly counterfeiter, it would be difficult to see the point of counterfeiting if each person is to receive the new money proportionately.

In real life, then, the very point of counterfeiting is to constitute a *process*, a process of transmitting new money from one pocket to another, and not the result of a magical and equi-proportionate expansion of money in everyone's pocket simultaneously. Whether counterfeiting is in the form of making brass or plastic coins that simulate gold, or of printing paper money to look like that of the government, counterfeiting is always a process in which the counterfeiter gets the new money *first*. This process was encapsulated in an old *New Yorker* cartoon, in which a group of counterfeiters are watching the first $10 bill emerge from their home printing press. One remarks: "Boy, is retail spending in the neighborhood in for a shot in the arm!"

And indeed it was. The first people who get the new money are the counterfeiters, which they then use to buy various goods and services. The second receivers of the new money are the retailers who sell those goods to the counterfeiters. And on and on the new money ripples out through the system, going from one pocket or till to another. As it does so, there is an immediate redistribution effect. For first the counterfeiters, then the retailers, etc., have new money and monetary income which they use to bid up goods and services, increasing their demand and raising the prices of the goods that they purchase. But as prices of goods begin to rise in response to the higher quantity of money, those who haven't yet received the new money find the prices of the goods they buy have gone up, while their own selling prices or incomes have not risen. In short, the early receivers of the new money in this market chain of events gain at the expense of those who receive the money toward the end of the chain, and still worse losers are the people (e.g., those on fixed incomes such as annuities, interest, or pensions) who never receive the new money at all. Monetary inflation, then, acts as a hidden "tax" by which the early receivers expropriate (i.e., gain at the expense of) the late receivers. And of course since the very earliest receiver of the new money is the counterfeiter, the counterfeiter's gain is the greatest. This tax is particularly insidious because it is hidden, because few people understand the processes of money and banking, and because it is all too easy to blame the rising prices, or "price inflation," caused by the monetary inflation on greedy capitalists, speculators, wild-spending consumers, or whatever social group is the easiest to denigrate. Obviously, too, it is to the interest of the counterfeiters to distract attention from their own crucial role by denouncing any and all other groups and institutions as responsible for the price inflation.

The inflation process is particularly insidious and destructive because everyone enjoys the feeling of having more money, while they generally complain about the consequences of more money, namely higher prices. But since there is an inevitable time lag between the stock of money increasing and its consequence in rising prices, and since the public has little knowledge of monetary economics, it is all too easy to fool it into placing the blame on shoulders far more visible than those of the counterfeiters.

The big error of all quantity theorists, from the British classicists to Milton Freidman, is to assume that money is only a "veil," and that increases in the quantity of money only have influence on the price level, or on the purchasing power of the money unit. On the contrary, it is one of the notable contributions of "Austrian School" economists and their predecessors, such as the early-eighteenth-century Irish-French economist Richard Cantillon, that, in addition to this quantitative, aggregative effect, an increase in the money supply also changes the distribution of income and wealth. The ripple effect also alters the structure of relative prices, and therefore of the kinds and quantities of goods that will be produced, since the counterfeiters and other early receivers will have different preferences and spending patterns from the late receivers who are "taxed" by the earlier receivers. Furthermore, these changes of income distribution, spending, relative prices, and production will be permanent and will not simply disappear, as the quantity theorists blithely assume, when the effects of the increase in the money supply will have worked themselves out.

In sum, the Austrian insight holds that counterfeiting will have far more unfortunate consequences for the economy than simple inflation of the price level. There will be other, and permanent, distortions of the economy away from the free market pattern that responds to consumers and property-rights holders in the free economy. This brings us to an important aspect of counterfeiting which should not be overlooked. In addition to its more narrowly economic distortion and unfortunate consequences, counterfeiting gravely cripples the moral and property rights foundation that lies at the base of any free-market economy.

Thus, consider a free-market society where gold is the money. In such a society, one can acquire money in only three ways: (a) by mining more gold; (b) by selling a good or service in exchange for gold owned by someone else; or (c) by receiving the gold as a voluntary gift or bequest from some other owner of gold. Each of these methods operates within a principle of strict defense of everyone's right to his private property. But say a counterfeiter appears on the scene. By creating fake gold coins he is able to acquire money in a fraudulent and coercive way, and with which he can enter the market to bid resources away from legitimate owners of gold. In that way, he robs current owners of gold just as surely, and even more massively, than if he burglarized their homes or safes. For this way, without actually breaking and entering the property of others, he can insidiously steal the fruits of their productive labor, and do so at the expense of all holders of money, and especially the later receivers of the new money.

Counterfeiting, therefore, is inflationary, redistributive, distorts the economic system, and amounts to stealthy and insidious robbery and expropriation of all legitimate property-owners in society.

Legalized Counterfeiting

Counterfeiters are generally reviled, and for good reason. One reason that gold and silver make good moneys is that they are easily recognizable, and are particularly difficult to simulate by counterfeits. "Coin-clipping," the practice of shaving edges off coins, was effectively stopped when the process of "milling" (putting vertical ridges onto the edges of coins) was developed. Private counterfeiting, therefore, has never been an important problem. But what happens when government sanctions, and in effect legalizes, counterfeiting, either by itself or by other institutions? Counterfeiting then becomes a grave economic and social problem indeed. For then there is no one to guard our guardians against their depredations of private property.

Historically, there have been two major kinds of legalized counterfeiting. One is *government paper money*. Under a gold standard, say that the currency unit in a society has become "one dollar," defined as 1/20 of an ounce of gold. At first, coins are minted with a certified weight of gold. Then, at one point, the first time in the North American colonies in

1690, a central government, perhaps because it is short of gold, decides to print paper tickets denominated in gold weights. At the beginning, the government prints the money as if it is equivalent to the weight of gold: a "ten dollar" ticket, or paper note, is so denominated because it implies equivalence to a "ten-dollar" gold coin, that is, a coin weighing 1/2 an ounce of gold. At first, the equivalence is maintained because the government promises redemption of this paper ticket in the same weight of gold whenever the ticket is presented to the government's Treasury. A "ten-dollar" note is pledged to be redeemable in 1/2 an ounce of gold. And at the beginning, if the government has little or no gold on hand, as was the case in Massachusetts in 1690, the explicit or implicit pledge is that very soon, in a year or two, the tickets *will be* redeemable in that weight of gold. And if the government is still trusted by the public, it might be able, at first, to pass these notes as equivalent to gold.

So long as the paper notes are treated on the market as equivalent to gold, the newly issued tickets add to the total money supply, and also serve to redistribute society's income and wealth. Thus, suppose that the government needs money quickly for whatever reason. It only has a stock of $2 million in gold on hand; it promptly issues $5 million in paper tickets, and spends it for whatever expenditure it deems necessary: say, in grants and loans to relatives of top government officials. Suppose, for example, the total gold stock outstanding in the country is $10 million, of which $2 million is in government hands; then, the issue of another $5 million in paper tickets increases the total quantity of money stock in the country by 50 percent. But the new funds are not proportionately distributed; on the contrary, the new $5 million goes first to the government. Then next to the relatives of officials, then to whomever sells goods and services to those relatives, and so on.

If the government falls prey to the temptation of printing a great deal of new money, not only will prices go up, but the "quality" of the money will become suspect in that society, and the lack of redeemability in gold may lead the market to accelerated discounting of that money in terms of gold. And if the money is not at all redeemable in gold, the rate of discount will accelerate further. In the American Revolution, the Continental Congress issued a great amount of non-redeemable paper dollars, which soon discounted radically, and in a few years, fell to such an enormous discount that they became literally worthless and disappeared from circulation. The common phrase "Not worth a Continental" became part of American folklore as a result of this runaway depreciation and accelerated worthlessness of the Continental dollars.

Loan Banking

Government paper, as pernicious as it may be, is a relatively straightforward form of counterfeiting. The public can understand the concept of "printing dollars" and spending them, and they can understand why such a flood of dollars will come to be worth a great deal less than gold, or than uninflated paper, of the same denomination, whether "dollar," "franc," or "mark." Far more difficult to grasp, however, and therefore far more insidious, are the nature and consequences of "fractional-reserve banking," a more subtle and modern form of counterfeiting. It is not difficult to see the consequences of a society awash in a flood of new paper money; but it is far more difficult to envision the results of an expansion of intangible bank credit.

One of the great problems in analyzing banking is that the word "bank" comprises several very different and even contradictory functions and operations. The ambiguity in the concept of "bank" can cover a multitude of sins. A bank, for example, can be considered "any institution that makes loans." The earliest "loan banks" were merchants who, in the natural course of trade, carried their customers by means of short-term credit, charging interest for the loans. The earliest bankers were "merchant-bankers," who began as merchants, and who, if they were successful at productive lending, gradually grew, like the great families the Riccis and the Medicis in Renaissance Italy, to become more bankers than merchants. It should be clear that these loans involved no inflationary creation of money. If the Medicis sold goods for 10 gold ounces and allowed their customers to pay in six months, including an interest premium, the total money supply was in no way increased. The Medici customers, instead of paying for the goods immediately, wait for several months, and then pay gold or silver with an additional fee for delay of payment.

This sort of loan banking is non-inflationary regardless of what the standard money is in the society, whether it be gold or government paper. Thus, suppose that in present-day America I set up a Rothbard Loan Bank. I save up $10,000 in cash and invest it as an asset of this new bank. My balance sheet, see Figure 1, which has assets on the left-hand side of a T-account, and the ownership of or claim to those assets on the right-hand side, the sum of which must be equal, now looks as follows:

Figure 1
A Bank Loan Begins

Rothbard Loan Bank

Assets	Equity + Liabilities
Cash: $10,000	
	Owned by Rothbard: $10,000
Total: $10,000	Total: $10,000

The bank is now ready for business; the $10,000 of cash assets is owned by myself.

Suppose, then, that $9,000 is loaned out to Joe at interest. The balance sheet will now look as follows in Figure 2.

The increased assets come from the extra $500 due as interest. The important point here is that money, whether it be gold or other standard forms of cash, has in no way increased; cash was saved up by me, loaned to Joe, who will then spend it, return it to me plus interest in the future, etc. The crucial point is that none of this banking has been inflationary, fraudulent, or counterfeit in any way. It has all been a normal, productive, entrepreneurial business

Figure 2
The Bank Makes Loans

Assets	Equity + Liabilities
Cash: $1,000 IOU from Joe: $9,500	Owned by Rothbard: $10,500
Total: $10,500	Total: $10,500

transaction. If Joe becomes insolvent and cannot repay, that would be a normal business or entrepreneurial failure.

If the Rothbard Bank, enjoying success, should expand the number of partners, or even incorporate to attract more capital, the business would expand, but the nature of this loan bank would remain the same; again, there would be nothing inflationary or fraudulent about its operations.

So far, we have the loan bank investing its own equity in its operations. Most people, however, think of "banks" as borrowing money from one set of people, and relending their money to another set, charging an interest differential because of its expertise in lending, in channeling capital to productive businesses. How would this sort of borrow-and-lend bank operate?

Let us take the Rothbard Loan Bank, as shown in Figure 3, and assume that the Bank borrows money from the public in the form of Certificates of Deposit (CDs), repayable in six months or a year. Then, abstracting from the interest involved, and assuming the Rothbard Bank floats $40,000 of CDs, and relends them, we will get a balance sheet as follows:

Figure 3
The Loan Bank Borrows Money

Assets	Equity + Liabilities
Cash: $1,000	Owed in CDs: $40,000
IOUs: $49,500	Owned by Rothbard: $10,500
Total: $50,500	Total: $50,500

Again, the important point is that the bank has grown, has borrowed and reloaned, and there has been no inflationary creation of new money, no fraudulent activity, and no counterfeiting. If the Rothbard Bank makes a bad loan, and becomes insolvent, then that is a normal entrepreneurial error. So far, loan banking has been a perfectly legitimate and productive activity.

Deposit Banking

We get closer to the nub of the problem when we realize that, historically, there has existed a very different type of "bank" that has no necessary logical connection, although it often had a practical connection, with loan banking. Gold coins are often heavy, difficult to carry around, and subject to risk of loss or theft. People began to "deposit" coins, as well as gold or silver bullion, into institutions for safekeeping. This function may be thought of as a "money-warehouse." As in the case of any other warehouse, the warehouse issues the depositor a receipt, a paper ticket pledging that the article will be redeemed at any time "on demand," that is, on presentation of the receipt. The receipt-holder, on presenting the ticket, pays a storage fee, and the warehouse returns the item.

The first thing to be said about this sort of deposit is that it would be very peculiar to say that the warehouse "owed" the depositor the chair or watch he had placed in its care, that the warehouse is the "debtor" and the depositor the "creditor." Suppose, for example, that you own a precious chair and that you place it in a warehouse for safekeeping over the summer. You return in the fall and the warehouseman says, "Gee, sorry, sir, but I've had business setbacks in the last few months, and I am not able to pay you the debt (the chair) that I owe you." Would you shrug your shoulders, and write the whole thing off as a "bad debt," as an unwise entrepreneurial decision on the part of the warehouseman? Certainly not. You would be properly indignant, for you do not regard placing the chair in a warehouse as some sort of "credit" or "loan" to the warehouseman. You do not lend the chair to him; you continue to own the chair, and you are placing it in his trust. He doesn't "owe" you the chair; the chair is and always continues to be yours; he is storing it for safekeeping. If the chair is not there when you arrive, you will call for the gendarmes and properly cry "theft!" You, and the law, regard the warehouseman who shrugs his shoulders at the absence of your chair not as someone who had made an unfortunate entrepreneurial error, but as a criminal who has absconded with your chair. More precisely, you and the law would charge the warehouseman with being an "embezzler," defined by *Webster's* as "one who appropriates fraudulently to one's own use what is entrusted to one's care and management."

Placing your goods in a warehouse (or, alternatively, in a safe-deposit box) is not, in other words, a "debt contract"; it is known in the law as a "bailment" contract, in which the bailor (the depositor) leaves property in the care, or in the trust of, the bailee (the warehouse). Furthermore, if a warehouse builds a reputation for probity, its receipts will circulate as equivalent to the actual goods in the warehouse. A warehouse receipt is of course payable to whomever holds the receipt; and so the warehouse receipt will be exchanged as if it were the good itself. If I buy your chair, I may not want to take immediate delivery of the chair itself. If I am familiar with the Jones Warehouse, I will accept the receipt for the chair at the Jones Warehouse as equivalent to receiving the actual chair. Just as a deed to a piece of land conveys title to the land itself, so does a warehouse receipt for a good serve as title to, or surrogate for, the good itself.[1]

Suppose you returned from your summer vacation and asked for your chair, and the warehouseman replied, "Well, sir, I haven't got your particular chair, but here's

---

[1]Thus, Armistead Dobie writes: "a transfer of the warehouse receipt, in general, confers the same measure of title that an actual delivery of the goods which it represents would confer." Armistead M. Dobie, *Handbook on the Law of Bailments and Carriers* (St. Paul, Minn.: West Publishing, 1914), p. 163.

another one just as good." You would be just about as indignant as before, and you would still call for the gendarmes: "I want my chair, dammit!" Thus, in the ordinary course of warehousing, the temptations to embezzle are strictly limited. Everyone wants his particular piece of property entrusted to your care, and you never know he they will want to redeem it.

Some goods, however, are of a special nature. They are homogeneous, so that no one unit can be distinguished from another. Such goods are known in law as being "fungible," where any unit of the good can replace any other. Grain is a typical example. If someone deposits 100,000 bushels of No. 1 wheat in a grain warehouse (known customarily as a "grain elevator"), all he cares about when redeeming the receipt is getting 100,000 bushels of that grade of wheat. He doesn't care whether these are the *same particular bushels* that he actually deposited in the elevator.

Unfortunately, this lack of caring about the specific items redeemed opens the door for a considerable amount of embezzlement by the warehouseowner. The warehouseman may now be tempted to think as follows: "While eventually the wheat will be redeemed and shipped to a flour mill, at any given time there is always a certain amount of unredeemed wheat in my warehouse. I therefore have a margin within which I can maneuver and profit by using someone else's wheat." Instead of carrying out his trust and his bailment contract by keeping all the grain in storage, he will be tempted to commit a certain degree of embezzlement. He is not very likely to actually drive off with or sell the wheat he has in storage. A more likely and more sophisticated form of defrauding would be for the grain elevator owner to *counterfeit* fake warehouse-receipts to, say, No. 1 wheat, and then lend out these receipts to speculators in the Chicago commodities market. The actual wheat in his elevator remains intact; but now he has printed fraudulent warehouse-receipts, receipts backed by nothing, ones that look exactly like the genuine article.

Honest warehousing, that is, one where every receipt is backed by a deposited good, may be referred to as "100 percent warehousing," that is, where every receipt is backed by the good for which it is supposed to be a receipt. On the other hand, if a warehouseman issues fake warehouse receipts, and the grain stored in his warehouse is only a fraction (or something less than 100 percent) of the receipts or paper tickets outstanding, then he may be said to be engaging in "fractional-reserve warehousing." It should also be clear that "fractional-reserve warehousing" is only a euphemism for fraud and embezzlement.

Writing in the late nineteenth century, the great English economist W. Stanley Jevons warned of the dangers of this kind of "general deposit warrant," where only a certain category of good is pledged for redemption of a receipt, in contrast to "specific deposit warrants," where the particular chair or watch must be redeemed by the warehouse. Using general warrants, "it becomes possible to create a fictitious supply of a commodity, that is, to make people believe that a supply exists which does not exist." On the other hand, with specific deposit warrants, such as "bills of lading, pawn-tickets, dock-warrants, or certificates which establish ownership to a definite object," it is not possible to issue such tickets "in excess of goods actually deposited, unless by distinct fraud." [2]

In the history of the U. S. grain market, grain elevators several times fell prey to this temptation, spurred by a lack of clarity in bailment law. Grain elevators issued fake warehouse receipts in grain during the 1860s, lent them to speculators in the Chicago wheat market, and caused dislocations in wheat prices and bankruptcies in the wheat market. Only a tightening of bailment law, ensuring that any issue of fake warehouse receipts is treated as fraudulent and illegal, finally put an end to this clearly impermissible practice. Unfortunately, however, this legal development did not occur in the vitally important field of warehouses for money, or deposit banking.

If "fractional-reserve" grain warehousing, that is, the issuing of warehouse receipts for non-existent goods, is clearly fraudulent, then so too is fractional-reserve warehousing for a good even more fungible than grain, i.e., money (whether it be gold or government paper). Any one unit of money is as good as any other, and indeed it is precisely for its homogeneity, divisibility, and recognizability that the market chooses gold as money in the first place. And in contrast to wheat, which after all, is eventually used to make flour and must therefore eventually be removed from the elevator, money, since it is used for exchange purposes only, does not *have* to be removed from the warehouse at all. Gold or silver may be removed for a non-monetary use

---

[2]W. Stanley Jevons, *Money and the Mechanism of Exchange*, 15th ed. (London: Kegan Paul, [1875] 1905), pp. 206–12.

such as jewelry, but paper money of course has only a monetary function, and therefore there is no compelling reason for warehouses ever to have to redeem their receipts. First, of course, the money-warehouse (also called a "deposit bank") must develop a market reputation for honesty and probity and for promptly redeeming their receipts whenever asked. But once trust has been built up, the temptation for the money-warehouse to embezzle, to commit fraud, can become overwhelming.

For at this point, the deposit banker may think to himself: "For decades, this bank has built up a brand name for honesty and for redeeming its receipts. By this time, only a small portion of my receipts are redeemed at all. People make money payments to each other in the market, but they exchange these warehouse receipts to money as if they were money (be it gold or government paper) itself. They hardly bother to redeem the receipts. Since my customers are such suckers, I can now engage in profitable hanky-panky and none will be the wiser."

The banker can engage in two kinds of fraud and embezzlement. He may, for example, simply take the gold or cash out of the vault and live it up, spending money on mansions or yachts. However, this may be a dangerous procedure; if he should ever be caught out, and people demand their money, the embezzling nature of his act might strike everyone as crystal-clear. Instead, a far more sophisticated and less blatant course will be for him to issue warehouse receipts to money, warehouse receipts backed by nothing but looking identical to the genuine receipts, and to lend them out to borrowers. In short, the banker counterfeits warehouse receipts to money, and lends them out. In that way, insofar as the counterfeiter is neither detected nor challenged to redeem in actual cash, the new fake receipts will, like the old genuine ones, circulate on the market as if they were money. Functioning as money, or money-surrogates, they will thereby add to the stock of money in the society, inflate prices, and bring about a redistribution of wealth and income from the late to the early receivers of the new "money."

If a banker has more room for fraud than a grain warehouseman, it should be clear that the consequences of his counterfeiting are far more destructive. Not just the grain market but all of society and the entire economy will be disrupted and harmed. As in the case of the coin counterfeiter, all property-owners, all owners of money, are expropriated and victimized by the counterfeiter, who is able to extract resources from the genuine producers by means of his fraud. And in the case of bank money, as we shall see further, the effect of the banker's depredations will not only be price inflation and redistribution of money and income, but also ruinous cycles of boom and bust generated by expansions and contractions of the counterfeit bank credit.

Problems for the Fractional-Reserve Banker: The Criminal Law

A deposit banker could not launch a career of "fractional-reserve" fraud and inflation from the start. If I have never opened a Rothbard Bank, I could not simply launch one and start issuing fraudulent warehouse-receipts. For who would take them? First, I would have to build up over the years a brand name for honest, 100-percent reserve banking; my career of fraud would have to be built parasitically upon my previous and properly built-up reputation for integrity and rectitude.

Once our banker begins his career of crime, there are several things he has to worry about. In the first place, he must worry that if he is caught out, he might go to jail and endure heavy fines as an embezzler. It becomes important for him to hire legal counsel, economists, and financial writers to convince the courts and the public that his fractional-reserve actions are certainly not fraud and embezzlement, that they are merely legitimate entrepreneurial actions and voluntary contracts. And that therefore if someone should present a receipt promising redemption in gold or cash on demand, and if the banker cannot pay, that this is merely an unfortunate entrepreneurial failure rather than the uncovering of a criminal act. To get away with this line of argument, he has to convince the authorities that his deposit liabilities are not a bailment, like a warehouse, but merely a good-faith debt. If the banker can convince people of this trickery, then he has greatly widened the temptation and the opportunity he enjoys, for practicing fractional-reserve embezzlement. It should be clear that, if the deposit banker, or money-warehouseman, is treated as a regular warehouseman, or bailee, the money deposited for his safe-keeping can never constitute part of the "asset" column on his balance sheet. In no sense can the money form part of his assets, and therefore in no sense are they a "debt" owed to the depositor to comprise part of the banker's liability column; as something stored for safekeeping, they are not loans or debts and therefore do not properly form part of his balance sheet at all.

Unfortunately, since bailment law was undeveloped in the nineteenth century, the bankers' counsel were able to swing the judicial decisions their way. The landmark decisions came in Britain in the first half of the nineteenth century, and these decisions were then taken over by the American courts. In the first important case, *Carr* v. *Carr*, in 1811, the British judge, Sir William Grant, ruled that since the money paid into a bank deposit had been paid generally, and not earmarked in a sealed bag (i.e., as a "specific deposit") that the transaction had become a loan rather than a bailment. Five years later, in the key follow-up case of *Devaynes* v. *Noble*, one of the counsel argued correctly that "a banker is rather a bailee of his customer's fund than his debtor, . . . because the money in . . . [his] hands is rather a deposit than a debt, and may therefore be instantly demanded and taken up." But the same Judge Grant again insisted that "money paid into a banker's becomes immediately a part of his general assets; and he is merely a debtor for the amount." In the final culminating case, *Foley* v. *Hill and Others*, decided by the House of Lords in 1848, Lord Cottenham, repeating the reasoning of the previous cases, put it lucidly if astonishingly:

> The money placed in the custody of a banker is, to all intents and purposes, the money of the banker, to do with as he pleases; he is guilty of no breach of trust in employing it; he is not answerable to the principal if he puts it into jeopardy, if he engages in a hazardous speculation; he is not bound to keep it or deal with it as the property of his principal; but

he is, of course, answerable for the amount, because he has contracted.[3]

The argument of Lord Cottenham and of all other apologists for fractional-reserve banking, that the banker only contracts for the amount of money, but not to keep the money on hand, ignores the fact that if all the depositors knew what was going on and exercised their claims at once, the banker *could not possibly* honor his commitments. In other words, honoring the contracts, and maintaining the entire system of fractional-reserve banking, requires a structure of smoke-and-mirrors, of duping the depositors into thinking that "their" money is safe, and would be honored should they wish to redeem their claims. The entire system of fractional-reserve banking, therefore, is built on deceit, a deceit connived at by the legal system.

A crucial question to be asked is this: why did grain warehouse law, where the conditions—of depositing fungible goods—are exactly the same, and grain is a general deposit and not an earmarked bundle—develop in precisely the opposite direction? Why did the courts finally recognize that deposits of even a fungible good, in the case of grain, are emphatically a bailment, not a debt? Could it be that the bankers conducted a more effective lobbying operation than did the grain men?

Indeed, the American courts, while adhering to the debt-not-bailment doctrine, have introduced puzzling anomalies

---

[3]See Murray N. Rothbard, *The Mystery of Banking* (New York: Richardson & Snyder, 1983), p. 94. On these decisions, see J. Milnes Holden, *The Law and Practice of Banking*, vol. 1, *Banker and Customer* (London: Pitman Publishing, 1970), pp. 31–32.

which indicate their confusion and hedging on this critical point. Thus, the authoritative law reporter Michie states that, in American law, a "bank deposit is more than an ordinary debt, and the depositor's relation to the bank is not identical to that of an ordinary creditor." Michie cites a Pennsylvania case, *People's Bank* v. *Legrand*, which affirmed that "a bank deposit is different from an ordinary debt in this, that from its very nature it is constantly subject to the check of the depositor, and is always payable on demand." Also, despite the law's insistence, following Lord Cottenham, that a bank "becomes the absolute owner of money deposited with it," yet a bank still "cannot speculate with its depositors' [?] money."[4]

Why aren't banks treated like grain elevators? That the answer is the result of politics rather than considerations of justice or property rights is suggested by the distinguished legal historian Arthur Nussbaum, when he asserts that adopting the "contrary view" (that a bank deposit is a bailment not a debt) would "lay an unbearable burden upon banking business." No doubt bank profits from the issue of fraudulent warehouse receipts would indeed come to an end as do any fraudulent profits when fraud is cracked down on. But grain elevators and other warehouses, after all, are able to remain in business successfully; why not genuine safe places for money?[5]

---

[4]A. Hewson Michie, *Michie on Banks and Banking*, rev. ed. (Charlottesville, Va.: Michie, 1973), 5A, pp. 1–31; and ibid., *1979 Cumulative Supplement*, pp. 3–9. See Rothbard, *The Mystery of Banking*, p. 275.

[5]The Bank of Amsterdam, which kept faithfully to 100-percent reserve banking from its opening in 1609 until it yielded to the temptation of financing Dutch wars in the late eighteenth century, financed itself by requiring depositors to renew their notes at the end of, say, a year, and

To highlight the essential nature of fractional-reserve banking, let us move for a moment away from banks that issue counterfeit warehouse receipts to cash. Let us assume, rather, that these deposit banks instead *actually print dollar bills* made up to look like the genuine article, replete with forged signatures by the Treasurer of the United States. The banks, let us say, print these bills and lend them out at interest. If they are denounced for what everyone would agree is forgery and counterfeiting, why couldn't these banks reply as follows: "Well, look, we do have genuine, non-counterfeit cash reserves of, say, 10 percent in our vaults. As long as people are willing to trust us, and accept these bills as equivalent to genuine cash, what's wrong with that? We are only engaged in a market transaction, no more nor less so than any other type of fractional-reserve banking." And what indeed is *wrong* about this statement that cannot be applied to any case of fractional-reserve banking?[6]

Problems for the Fractional-Reserve Banker: Insolvency

This unfortunate turn of the legal system means that the fractional-reserve banker, even if he violates his contract, cannot be treated as an embezzler and a criminal; but the banker must still face the lesser, but still unwelcome fact of insolvency. There are two major ways in which he can become insolvent.

---

then charging a fee for the renewal. See Arthur Nussbaum, *Money in the Law: National and International* (Brooklyn: Foundation Press, 1950), p. 105.

[6]I owe this point to Dr. David Gordon. See Murray N. Rothbard, *The Present State of Austrian Economics* (Auburn, Ala.: Ludwig von Mises Institute Working Paper, November 1992), p. 36.

The first and most devastating route, because it could happen at any time, is if the bank's customers, those who hold the warehouse receipts or receive it in payment, lose confidence in the chances of the bank's repayment of the receipts and decide, *en masse*, to cash them in. This loss of confidence, if it spreads from a few to a large number of bank depositors, is devastating because it is always fatal. It is fatal because, by the very nature of fractional-reserve banking, the bank *cannot honor* all of its contracts. Hence the overwhelming nature of the dread process known as a "bank run," a process by which a large number of bank customers get the wind up, sniff trouble, and demand their money. The "bank run," which shivers the timbers of every banker, is essentially a "populist" uprising by which the duped public, the depositors, demand the right to their own money. This process can and will break any bank subject to its power. Thus, suppose that an effective and convincing orator should go on television tomorrow, and urge the American public: "People of America, the banking system of this country is insolvent. 'Your money' is not in the bank vaults. They have less than 10 percent of your money on hand. People of America, get your money out of the banks *now* before it is too late!" If the people should now heed this advice *en masse*, the American banking system would be destroyed tomorrow.[7]

A bank's "customers" are comprised of several groups. They are those people who make the initial deposit of cash (whether gold or government paper money) in a bank. They

___

[7]This holocaust could only be stopped by the Federal Reserve and Treasury simply printing all the cash demanded and giving it to the banks—but that would precipitate a firestorm of runaway inflation.

are, in the second place, those who borrow the bank's counterfeit issue of warehouse receipts. But they are *also* a great number of other people, specifically those who *accept* the bank's receipts in exchange, who thereby become a bank's customers in that sense.

Let us see how the fractional-reserve process works. Because of the laxity of the law, a deposit of cash in a bank is treated as a credit rather than a bailment, and the loans go on the bank's balance sheet. Let us assume, first, that I set up a Rothbard Deposit Bank, and that at first this bank adheres strictly to a 100-percent reserve policy. Suppose that $20,000 is deposited in the bank. Then, abstracting from my capital and other assets of the bank, its balance sheet will look as in Figure 4:

Figure 4
One-Hundred Percent Reserve Banking

Rothbard Deposit Bank

Assets	Equity + Liabilities
Cash: $20,000	Warehouse Receipts to Cash: $20,000

So long as Rothbard Bank receipts are treated by the market as if they are equivalent to cash, and they function as such, the receipts will function instead of, *as surrogates for*, the actual cash. Thus, suppose that Jones had deposited $3,000 at the Rothbard Bank. He buys a painting from an art gallery and pays for it with his deposit receipt of $3,000. (The receipt, as we shall see, can either be a written ticket or an open book account.) If the art gallery wishes, it need not bother redeeming the receipt for cash; it can treat the receipt as if it were cash, and itself hold on to the receipt. The art gallery then becomes a "customer" of the Rothbard Bank.

It should be clear that, in our example, either the cash itself *or* the receipt to cash circulates as money: never both at once. So long as deposit banks adhere strictly to 100-percent reserve banking, there is no increase in the money supply; only the *form* in which the money circulates changes. Thus, if there are $2 million of cash existing in a society, and people deposit $1.2 million in deposit banks, then the total of $2 million of money remains the same; the only difference is that $800,000 will continue to be cash, whereas the remaining $1.2 million will circulate as warehouse receipts to the cash.

Suppose now that banks yield to the temptation to create fake warehouse receipts to cash, and lend these fake receipts out. What happens now is that the previously strictly separate functions of loan and deposit banking become muddled; the deposit trust is violated, and the deposit contract cannot be fulfilled if all the "creditors" try to redeem their claims. The phony warehouse receipts are loaned out by the bank. Fractional-reserve banking has reared its ugly head.

Thus, suppose that the Rothbard Deposit Bank in the previous table decides to create $15,000 in fake warehouse receipts, unbacked by cash, but redeemable on demand in cash, and lends them out in various loans or purchases of securities. For how the Rothbard Bank's balance sheet now looks see Figure 5:

Figure 5
Fractional-Reserve Banking

Rothbard Deposit Bank

Assets	Equity + Liabilities
Cash: $20,000	Warehouse Receipts to Cash: $35,000
IOUs from Debtors: $15,000	
Total: $35,000	Total: $35,000

In this case, something very different has happened in a bank's lending operation. There is again an increase in warehouse receipts circulating as money, and a relative decline in the use of cash, but in this case there has also been a *total increase* in the supply of money. The money supply has increased because warehouse receipts have been issued that are redeemable in cash but not fully backed by cash. As in the case of any counterfeiting, the result, so long as the warehouse receipts function as surrogates for cash, will be to increase the money supply in the society, to raise prices of goods in terms of dollars, and to redistribute money and wealth to the early receivers of the new bank money (in the first instance, the bank itself, and then its debtors, and those whom the latter spend the money on) at the expense of those who receive the new bank money later or not at all. Thus, if the society starts with $800,000 circulating as cash and $1.2 million circulating as warehouse receipts, as in the previous example, and the banks issue another $1.7 million in phony warehouse receipts, the total money supply will increase from $2 million to $3.7 million, of which $800,000 will still be in cash, with $2.9 million now in warehouse receipts, of which $1.2 million are backed by actual cash in the banks.

Are there any limits on this process? Why, for example, does the Rothbard Bank stop at a paltry $15,000, or do the banks as a whole stop at $1.7 million? Why doesn't the Rothbard Bank seize a good thing and issue $500,000 or more, or umpteen millions, and the banks as a whole do likewise? What is to stop them?

The answer is the fear of insolvency; and the most devastating route to insolvency, as we have noted, is the bank run. Suppose, for example, that the banks go hog wild: the Rothbard Bank issues many millions of fake warehouse receipts; the banking system as a whole issues hundreds of millions. The more the banks issue beyond the cash in their vaults, the more outrageous the discrepancy, and the greater the possibility of a sudden loss of confidence in the banks, a loss that may start in one group or area and then, as bank runs proliferate, spread like wildfire throughout the country. And the greater the possibility for someone to go on TV and warn the public of this growing danger. And once a bank run gets started, there is nothing in the market economy that can stop that run short of demolishing the entire jerry-built fractional-reserve banking system in its wake.

Apart from and short of a bank run, there is another powerful check on bank credit expansion under fractional reserves, a limitation that applies to expansion *by any one particular* bank. Let us assume, for example, an especially huge expansion of pseudo-warehouse receipts by one bank. Suppose that the Rothbard Deposit Bank, previously hewing to 100-percent reserves, decides to make a quick killing and go all-out: upon a cash reserve of $20,000, previously backing receipts of $20,000, it decides to print unbacked warehouse receipts of $1,000,000, lending them out at interest to various borrowers. Now the Rothbard Bank's balance sheet will be as in Figure 6:

Figure 6
One Bank's Hyper-Expansion

Rothbard Deposit Bank

Assets	Liabilities
Cash: $20,000	Warehouse Receipts to Cash: $1,020,000
IOUs from people: $1,000,000	
Total: $1,020,000	Total: $1,020,000

Everything may be fine and profitable for the Rothbard Bank for a brief while, but there is now one enormous fly embedded in its ointment. Suppose that the Rothbard Bank creates and lends out fake receipts of $1,000,000 to one firm, say the Ace Construction Company. The Ace Construction Company, of course, is not going to borrow money and pay interest on it but not use it; quickly, it will pay out these receipts in exchange for various goods and services. If the persons or firms who receive the receipts from Ace are all customers of the Rothbard Bank, then all is fine; the receipts are simply passed back and forth from one of the Rothbard Bank's customers to another. But suppose, instead, that the receipts go to people who are *not* customers of the Rothbard Bank, or not bank customers at all.

Suppose, for example, that the Ace Construction Company pays $1 million to the Curtis Cement Company. And the Curtis Cement Company, for some reason, doesn't use banks; it presents the receipt for $1 million to the Rothbard Bank and demands redemption. What happens? The Rothbard Bank, of course, has peanuts, or more precisely, $20,000. It is immediately insolvent and out of business.

More plausibly, let us suppose that the Curtis Cement Company uses a bank, all right, but not the Rothbard Bank. In that case, say, the Curtis Cement Company presents the $1 million receipt to its own bank, the World Bank, and the World Bank presents the receipt for $1 million to the Rothbard Bank and demands cash. The Rothbard Bank, of course, doesn't have the money, and again is out of business.

Note that for an individual expansionist bank to inflate warehouse receipts excessively and go out of business does *not* require a bank run; it doesn't even require that the person who eventually receives the receipts is not a customer of banks. This person need only present the receipt to *another* bank to create trouble for the Rothbard Bank that cannot be overcome.

For any one bank, the more it creates fake receipts, the more danger it will be in. But more relevant will be the number of its banking competitors and the extent of its own clientele in relation to other competing banks. Thus, if the Rothbard Bank is the only bank in the country, then there are no limits imposed on its expansion of receipts *by competition*; the only limits become either a bank run or a general unwillingness to use bank money at all.

On the other hand, let us ponder the opposite if unrealistic extreme: that every bank has *only one* customer, and that therefore there are millions of banks in a country. In that case, *any* expansion of unbacked warehouse receipts will be impossible, regardless how small. For then, even a small expansion by the Rothbard Bank beyond its cash in the vaults will lead very quickly to a demand for redemption by another bank which cannot be honored, and therefore insolvency.

One force, of course, could overcome this limit of calls for redemption by competing banks: a cartel agreement among all banks to accept each other's receipts and not call on their fellow banks for redemption. While there are many reasons for banks to engage in such cartels, there are also difficulties, difficulties which multiply as the number of banks becomes larger. Thus, if there are only three or four banks in a country, such an agreement would be relatively simple. One problem in expanding banks is making sure that all banks expand relatively proportionately. If there are a number of banks in a country, and Banks A and B expand wildly while the other banks only expand their receipts a little, claims on Banks A and B will pile up rapidly in the vaults of the other banks, and the temptation will be to bust these two banks and not let them get away with relatively greater profits. The fewer the number of competing banks in existence, the easier it will be to coordinate rates of expansion. If there are many thousands of banks, on the other hand, coordination will become very difficult and a cartel agreement is apt to break down.[8]

Booms and Busts

We have so far emphasized that bank credit expansion under fractional-reserve banking (or "creation of counterfeit warehouse receipts") creates price inflation, loss of purchasing power of the currency unit, and redistribution of wealth and income. Euphoria caused by a pouring of new money into the economy is followed by grumbling as price inflation sets in, and some people benefit while others lose. But inflationary booms are not the only consequence of fractional-reserve counterfeiting. For at some point in the process, a reaction sets in. An actual bank run might set in, sweeping across the

---

[8]An example of a successful cartel for bank credit expansion occurred in Florence in the second half of the sixteenth century. There, the Ricci bank was the dominant bank among a half dozen or so others, and was able to lead a tight cartel of banks that took in and paid out each other's receipts without bothering to redeem in specie. The result was a large expansion and an ensuing long-time bank crisis. Carlo M. Cipolla, *Money in Sixteenth-Century Florence* (Berkeley and Los Angeles: University of California Press, 1987), pp. 101–13.

It is likely that the establishment of the Bank of Amsterdam in 1609, followed by other 100 percent reserve banks in Europe, was a reaction against such bank credit-generated booms and busts as had occurred in Florence not many years earlier.

banking system; or banks, in fear of such a run, might suddenly contract their credit, call in and not renew their loans, and sell securities they own, in order to stay solvent. This sudden contraction will also swiftly contract the amount of warehouse receipts, or money, in circulation. In short, as the fractional-reserve system is either found out or in danger of being found out, swift credit contraction leads to a financial and business crisis and recession. There is no space here to go into a full analysis of business cycles, but it is clear that the credit-creation process by the banks habitually generates destructive boom-bust cycles.[9]

Types of Warehouse Receipts

Two kinds of warehouse receipts for deposit banks have developed over the centuries. One is the regular form of receipt, familiar to anyone who has ever used any sort of warehouse: a paper ticket in which the warehouse guarantees to hand over, on demand, the particular product mentioned on the receipt, e.g., "The Rothbard Bank will pay to the bearer of this ticket on demand," 10 dollars in gold coin, or Treasury paper money, or whatever. For deposit banks, this is called a "note" or "bank note." Historically, the bank note is the overwhelmingly dominant form of warehouse receipt.

Another form of deposit receipt, however, emerged in the banks of Renaissance Italy. When a merchant was large-scale and very well-known, he and the bank found it more

---

[9]For more on business cycles, see Murray N. Rothbard, "The Positive Theory of the Cycle," in *America's Great Depression*, 4th ed. (New York: Richardson & Snyder, 1983), pp. 11–38.

convenient for the warehouse receipt to be invisible, that is, to remain as an "open book account" on the books of the bank. Then, if he paid large sums to another merchant, he did not have to bother transferring actual bank notes; he would just write out a transfer order to his bank to shift some of his open book account to that of the other merchant. Thus, Signor Medici might write out a transfer order to the Ricci Bank to transfer 100,000 lira of his open book account at the Bank to Signor Bardi. This transfer order has come to be known as a "check," and the open book deposit account at the bank as a "demand deposit," or "checking account." Note the form of the contemporary transfer order known as a check: "I, Murray N. Rothbard, direct the Bank of America to pay to the account of Service Merchandise 100 dollars."

It should be noted that the bank note and the open book demand deposit are economically and legally equivalent. Each is an alternative form of warehouse receipt, and each takes its place in the total money supply as a surrogate, or substitute, for cash. However, the check itself is not the equivalent of the bank note, even though both are paper tickets. The bank note itself is the warehouse receipt, and therefore the surrogate, or substitute for cash and a constituent of the supply of money in the society. The check is not the warehouse receipt itself, but an order to transfer the receipt, which is an intangible open book account on the books of the bank.

If the receipt-holder chooses to keep his receipts in the form of a note or a demand deposit, or shifts from one to another, it should make no difference to the bank or to the total supply of money, whether the bank is practicing 100-percent or fractional-reserve banking.

But even though the bank note and the demand deposit are economically equivalent, the two forms will not be equally marketable or acceptable on the market. The reason is that while a merchant or another bank must always trust the bank in question in order to accept its note, for a check to be accepted the receiver must trust not only the bank but also the person who signs the check. In general, it is far easier for a bank to develop a reputation and trust in the market economy, than for an individual depositor to develop an equivalent brand name. Hence, wherever banking has been free and relatively unregulated by government, checking accounts have been largely confined to wealthy merchants and businessmen who have themselves developed a widespread reputation. In the days of uncontrolled banking, checking deposits were held by the Medicis or the Rockefellers or their equivalent, not by the average person in the economy. If banking were to return to relative freedom, it is doubtful if checking accounts would continue to dominate the economy.

For wealthy businessmen, however, checking accounts may yield many advantages. Checks will not have to be accumulated in fixed denominations, but can be made out for a precise and a large single amount; and unlike a loss of bank notes in an accident or theft, a loss of check forms will not entail an actual decline in one's assets.

Enter the Central Bank

Central Banking began in England, when the Bank of England was chartered in 1694. Other large nations copied this institution over the next two centuries, the role of the Central Bank reaching its now familiar form with the English Peel

Act of 1844. The United States was the last major nation to enjoy the dubious blessings of Central Banking, adopting the Federal Reserve System in 1913.

The Central Bank was privately owned, at least until it was generally nationalized after the mid-twentieth century. But it has always been in close cahoots with the central government. The Central Bank has always had two major roles: (1) to help finance the government's deficit; and (2) to cartelize the private commercial banks in the country, so as to help remove the two great market limits on their expansion of credit, on their propensity to counterfeit: a possible loss of confidence leading to bank runs; and the loss of reserves should any one bank expand its own credit. For cartels on the market, even if they are to each firm's advantage, are very difficult to sustain unless government enforces the cartel. In the area of fractional-reserve banking, the Central Bank can assist cartelization by removing or alleviating these two basic free-market limits on banks' inflationary expansion credit.

It is significant that the Bank of England was launched to help the English government finance a large deficit. Governments everywhere and at all times are short of money, and much more desperately so than individuals or business firms. The reason is simple: unlike private persons or firms, who obtain money by selling needed goods and services to others, governments produce nothing of value and therefore have nothing to sell.[10] Governments can only obtain money

---

[10]A minor exception: when admirably small governments such as Monaco or Liechtenstein issue beautiful stamps to be purchased by

by grabbing it from others, and therefore they are always on the lookout to find new and ingenious ways of doing the grabbing. Taxation is the standard method; but, at least until the twentieth century, the people were very edgy about taxes, and any increase in a tax or imposition of a new tax was likely to land the government in revolutionary hot water.

After the discovery of printing, it was only a matter of time until governments began to "counterfeit" or to issue paper money as a substitute for gold or silver. Originally the paper was redeemable or supposedly redeemable in those metals, but eventually it was cut off from gold so that the currency unit, the dollar, pound, mark, etc. became names for independent tickets or notes issued by government rather than units of weight of gold or silver. In the Western world, the first government paper money was issued by the British colony of Massachusetts in 1690.[11]

The 1690s were a particularly difficult time for the English government. The country had just gone through four decades of revolution and civil war, in large part in opposition to high taxes, and the new government scarcely felt secure enough to impose a further bout of higher taxation. And yet, the government had many lands it wished to conquer, especially the mighty French Empire, a feat that would

---

collectors. Sometimes, of course, governments will seize and monopolize a service or resource and sell their products (e.g., a forest) or sell the monopoly rights to its production, but these are scarcely exceptions to the eternal coercive search for revenue by government.

[11]Printing was first developed in ancient China, and so it should come as no surprise that the first government paper money arrived in mid-eighth century China. See Gordon Tullock, "Paper Money—A Cycle in Cathay," *Economic History Review* 9, no. 3 (1957): 396.

entail a vast increase in expenditures. The path of deficit spending seemed blocked for the English since the government had only recently destroyed its own credit by defaulting on over half of its debt, thereby bankrupting a large number of capitalists in the realm, who had entrusted their savings to the government. Who then would lend anymore money to the English State?

At this difficult juncture, Parliament was approached by a syndicate headed by William Paterson, a Scottish promoter. The syndicate would establish a Bank of England, which would print enough bank notes, supposedly payable in gold or silver, to finance the government deficit. No need to rely on voluntary savings when the money tap could be turned on! In return, the government would keep all of its deposits at the new bank. Opening in July 1694, the Bank of England quickly issued the enormous sum of £760,000, most of which was used to purchase government debt. In less than two years time, the bank's outstanding notes of £765,000 were only backed by £36,000 in cash. A run demanding specie smashed the bank, which was now out of business. But the English government, in the first of many such bailouts, rushed in to allow the Bank of England to "suspend specie payments," that is, to cease its obligations to pay in specie, while yet being able to force *its* debtors to pay the bank in full. Specie payments resumed two years later, but from then on, the government allowed the Bank of England to suspend specie payment, while continuing in operation, every time it got into financial difficulties.

The year following the first suspension, in 1697, the Bank of England induced Parliament to prohibit any new corporate bank from being established in England. In other words, no other incorporated bank could enter into competition with the Bank. In addition, counterfeiting Bank of England notes was now made punishable by death. A decade later, the government moved to grant the Bank of England a virtual monopoly on the issue of bank notes. In particular, after 1708, it was unlawful for any corporation other than the Bank of England to issue paper money, and any note issue by bank partnerships of more than six persons was also prohibited.

The modern form of Central Banking was established by the Peel Act of 1844. The Bank of England was granted an absolute monopoly on the issue of all bank notes in England. These notes, in turn, were redeemable in gold. Private commercial banks were only allowed to issue demand deposits. This meant that, in order to acquire cash demanded by the public, the banks had to keep checking accounts at the Bank of England. In effect, bank demand deposits were redeemable in Bank of England notes, which in turn were redeemable in gold. There was a double-inverted pyramid in the banking system. At the bottom pyramid, the Bank of England, engaging in fractional-reserve banking, multiplied fake warehouse receipts to gold—its notes and deposits—on top of its gold reserves. In their turn, in a second inverted pyramid on top of the Bank of England, the private commercial banks pyramided their demand deposits on top of *their* reserves, or their deposit accounts, at the Bank of England. It is clear that, once Britain went off the gold standard, first during World War I and finally in 1931, the Bank of England notes could serve as the standard fiat money, and the private banks could still pyramid demand deposits on top of their Bank of England reserves. The big difference is that now the gold standard no longer served as any kind of check upon the Central Bank's expansion of its credit, i.e., its counterfeiting of notes and deposits.

Note, too, that with the prohibition of private bank issue of *notes*, in contrast to demand deposits, for the first time the *form* of warehouse receipt, whether notes or deposits, made a big difference. If bank customers wish to hold cash, or paper notes, instead of intangible deposits, their banks have to go to the Central Bank and draw down their reserves. As we shall see later in analyzing the Federal Reserve, the result is that a change from demand deposit to note has a contractionary effect on the money supply, whereas a change from note to intangible deposit will have an inflationary effect.

Easing the Limits on
Bank Credit Expansion

The institution of Central Banking eased the free-market restrictions on fractional-reserve banking in several ways. In the first place, by the mid-nineteenth century a "tradition" was craftily created that the Central Bank must always act as a "lender of last resort" to bail out the banks should the bulk of them get into trouble. The Central Bank had the might, the law, and the prestige of the State behind it; it was the depository of the State's accounts; and it had the implicit promise that the State regards the Central Bank as "too big to fail." Even under the gold standard, the Central Bank note tended to be used, at least implicitly, as legal tender, and actual redemption in gold, at least by domestic citizens, was increasingly discouraged though not actually prohibited. Backed by the Central Bank and beyond it by the State itself, then, public confidence in the banking system was artificially bolstered, and runs on the banking system became far less likely.

Even under the gold standard, then, domestic demands for gold became increasingly rare, and there was generally little for the banks to worry about. The major problem for the bankers was *international* demands for gold, for while the citizens of, say, France, could be conned into not demanding gold for notes or deposits, it was difficult to dissuade British or German citizens holding bank deposits in francs from cashing them in for gold.

The Peel Act system insured that the Central Bank could act as a cartelizing device, and in particular to make sure that the severe free-market limits on the expansion *of any one bank* could be circumvented. In a free market, as we remember, if a Rothbard Bank expanded notes or deposits by itself, these warehouse receipts would quickly fall into the hands of clients *of other banks*, and these people or their banks would demand redemption of Rothbard warehouse receipts in gold. And since the whole point of fractional-reserve banking is *not* to have sufficient money to redeem the receipts, the Rothbard Bank would quickly go under. But if a Central Bank enjoys the monopoly of bank notes, and the commercial banks all pyramid expansion of their demand deposits on top of their "reserves," or checking accounts at the Central Bank, then all the Bank need do to assure successful cartelization is to expand proportionately throughout the country, so that all competing banks increase their reserves, and can expand together at the same rate. Then, if the Rothbard Bank, for example, prints warehouse receipts far beyond, say triple, its reserves in deposits at the Central Bank, it will not, on net, lose reserves if all the competing banks are expanding *their* credit at the same rate. In this way, the Central Bank acts as an effective cartelizing agent.

But while the Central Bank can mobilize all the banks within a country and make sure they all expand the money-substitutes they create at the same rate, they once again have a problem with the banks of *other* countries. While the Central Bank of Ruritania can see to it that all the Ruritanian banks are mobilized and expand their credit and the money-supply together, it has no power over the banks or the currencies of other countries. Its cartelizing potential extends only to the borders of its own country.

The Central Bank Buys Assets

Before analyzing operations of the Federal Reserve in more detail, we should understand that the most important way that a Central Bank can cartelize its banking system is by increasing the reserves of the banks, and the most important way to do that is simply by buying assets.

In a gold standard, the "reserve" of a commercial bank, the asset that allegedly stands behind its notes or deposits, is gold. When the Central Bank enters the scene, and particularly after the Peel Act of 1844, the reserves consist of gold, but predominantly they consist of the bank's demand deposit account at the Central Bank, an account which enables the bank to redeem its own checking account in the notes of the Central Bank, which enjoys a State-granted monopoly on the issue of tangible notes. As a result, in practice the banks hold Central Bank deposits as their reserve and they redeem in Central Bank notes, whereas the Central Bank is pledged to redeem those notes in gold.

This post–Peel Act structure, it is clear, not undesignedly paved the way for a smooth transition to a fiat paper standard. Since the average citizen had come to use Central Bank notes as his cash, and gold was demanded only by foreigners, it was relatively easy and not troublesome for the government to go off gold and to refuse to redeem its or its Central Bank notes in specie. The average citizen continued to use Bank notes and the commercial banks continued to redeem their deposits in those notes. The daily economic life of the country seemed to go on much as before. It should be clear that, if there had been no Central Bank, and especially no Central Bank with a Peel Act type monopoly of notes, going off gold would have created a considerable amount of trouble and a public outcry.

How, then, can the Central Bank increase the reserves of the banks under its jurisdiction? Simply by buying assets. It doesn't matter *whom* it buys assets from, whether from the banks or from any other individual or firm in the economy. Suppose a Central Bank buys an asset from a bank. For example, the Central Bank buys a building, owned by the Jonesville Bank for $1,000,000. The building, appraised at $1,000,000, is transferred from the asset column of the Jonesville Bank to the asset column of the Central Bank. How does the Central Bank pay for the building? Simple: by writing out a check on itself for $1,000,000. Where did it get the money to write out the check? It created the money out of thin air, i.e., by creating a fake warehouse receipt for $1,000,000 in cash which it does not possess. The Jonesville Bank deposits the check at the Central Bank, and the Jonesville Bank's deposit account at the Central Bank goes up by $1,000,000. The Jonesville Bank's total reserves have increased by $1,000,000, upon which it and other banks will be able, in a short period of time, to multiply their own warehouse receipts to non-existent reserves manyfold, and thereby to increase the money supply of the country manyfold.

Figure 7 demonstrates this initial process of purchasing assets. We now have to deal with two sets of T-accounts: the commercial bank and the Central Bank The process is shown as in figure 7.

Figure 7
Central Bank Buys an Asset from a Commercial Bank

Commercial Bank

Assets	Equity + Liabilities
House: $1,000,000 Deposit at Central Bank: + $1,000,000	

Central Bank

Assets	Equity + Liabilities
House: + $1,000,000	Deposit to banks: + $1,000,000

Now, let us analyze the similar, though less obvious, process that occurs when the Central Bank buys an asset from anyone, any individual or firm, in the economy. Suppose that the Central Bank buys a house worth $1,000,000 from Jack Levitt, homebuilder. The Central Bank's asset column increases by $1,000,000 for the house; again, it pays for the house by writing a $1,000,000 check on itself, a warehouse receipt for non-existent cash it creates out of thin air. It writes out the check to Mr. Levitt. Levitt, who cannot have an account at the Central Bank (only banks can do so), can do only one thing with the check: deposit it at whatever bank he uses. This increases his checking account by $1,000,000. Now, here there is a variant on the events of the previous example. Already, in the one act of depositing this check, the total money supply in the country has increased by $1,000,000, a $1,000,000 which did not exist before. So an inflationary increase in the money supply has already occurred. And redistribution has already occurred as well, since all of the new money, at least initially, resides in the possession of Mr. Levitt. But this is only the initial increase, for the bank used by Levitt, say the Rockville Bank, takes the check and deposits it at the Central Bank, thereby gaining $1,000,000 in its deposits, which serve as its reserves for its own fractional-reserve banking operations. The Rockville Bank, accompanied by other, competing banks, will then be able to pyramid an expansion of multiple amounts of warehouse receipts and credits, which will comprise the new warehouse receipts being loaned out. There will be a multiple expansion of the money supply. This process can be seen in Figures 8 and 9 below.

At this point, the commercial bank has an increase in its reserves—its demand deposits at the Central Bank—of $1,000,000. This bank, accompanied by its fellow commercial banks, can now expand a multiple of loans and demand deposits on top of those reserves. Let us assume—a fairly realistic assumption—that that multiple is 10-to-1. The bank feels that now it can expand its demand deposits to 10 times its reserves. It now creates new demand deposits in the process of lending them out to businesses or consumers, either directly or in the course of purchasing securities on the

---

Figure 8
Central Bank Buys an Asset from a Non-Bank

Commercial Bank

Assets	Equity + Liabilities
Demand deposit at Central Bank: + $1,000,000	Demand deposits: (to Levitt) + $1,000,000

Central Bank

Assets	Equity + Liabilities
House: + $1,000,000	Demand deposits to banks: + $1,000,000

market. At the end of this expansion process taking a few weeks, the bank's balance sheet can be seen in Figure 9 below. Note that the situation in Figure 9 could have resulted, either from the direct purchase of an asset by the Central Bank from the commercial bank itself (Figure 7), *or* by purchasing an asset in the open market from someone who is a depositor at this or another commercial bank (Figure 8). The end result will be the same.

Figure 9

Result of Credit Expansion Process

Commercial Banks

Assets	Equity + Liabilities
IOUs due from business: + $9,000,000	Demand deposits: + $10,000,000
Demand deposit at Central Bank: + $1,000,000	

Central Bank

Assets	Equity + Liabilities
House: + $1,000,000	Demand deposits to banks: + $1,000,000

Origins of the Federal Reserve:
The Advent of the National Banking System

It should now be crystal clear what the attitude of commercial banks is and almost always will be toward the Central Bank in their country. The Central Bank is their support, their staff and shield against the winds of competition and of people trying to obtain money which they believe to be their own property waiting in the banks' vaults. The Central Bank crucially bolsters the confidence of the gulled public in the banks and deters runs upon them. The Central Bank is the banks' lender of last resort, and the cartelizer that enables all the banks to expand together so that one set of banks doesn't lose reserves to another and is forced to contract sharply or go under. The Central Bank is almost critically necessary to the prosperity of the commercial banks, to their professional career as manufacturers of new money through issuing illusory warehouse receipts to standard cash.

Also we can now see the mendacity of the common claim that private commercial banks are "inflation hawks" or that Central Banks are eternally guarding the pass against inflation. Instead, they are all jointly the inflation-creators, and the *only* inflation-creators, in the economy.

Now this does not mean, of course, that banks are never griping about their Central Bank. In every "marriage" there is friction, and there is often grousing by the banks against their shepherd and protector. But the complaint, almost always, is that the Central Bank is not inflating, is not protecting them, intensely or consistently *enough*. The Central Bank, while the leader and mentor of the commercial banks, must also consider other pressures, largely political. Even when, as now, their notes are standard cash, they must worry about public opinion, or about populist complaints against inflation, or about instinctively shrewd if often unsophisticated public denunciations of the "money power." The attitude of a bank toward the Central Bank and government is akin to general bellyaching by welfare "clients" or by industries seeking subsidies, against the government. The complaints are almost always directed, not against the existence of the welfare system or the subsidy program, but against alleged "deficiencies" in the intensity and scope of the subventions. Ask the complainers if they wish to abolish welfare or subsidies and you will see the horror of their response, if indeed they can be induced to treat the question seriously. In the same way, ask any bankers if they wish to abolish their Central Bank and the reaction of horror will be very similar.[12]

For the first century of the history of the American Republic, money and banking were crucial policy issues between the political parties. A Central Bank was a live issue from the beginning of the American nation. At each step of

---

[12]It is a commonly accepted myth that the "state banks" (the state-chartered private commercial banks) strongly supported Andrew Jackson's abolition of the Second Bank of the United States—the Central Bank of that time. However (apart from the fact that this was a pre-Peel Act Central Bank that did not have a monopoly on bank notes and hence competed with commercial banks as well as providing reserves for their expansion) this view is sheer legend, based on the faulty view of historians that since the state banks were supposedly "restrained " in their expansion by the Bank of the United States, they *must* have favored its abolition. On the contrary, as later historians have shown, the overwhelming majority of the banks supported retention of the Bank of the United States, as our analysis would lead us to predict. See John M. McFaul, *The Politics of Jacksonian Finance* (Ithaca, N.Y.: Cornell University Press, 1972), pp. 16–57; and Jean Alexander Wilburn, *Biddle's Bank: The Crucial Years* (New York: Columbia University Press, 1970), pp. 118–19.

the way, the champions of the Central Bank were the enthusiastic Nationalists, the advocates of a Big Central Government. In fact, in 1781, even before the Revolutionary War was over, the leading Nationalist, Philadelphia's merchant tycoon Robert Morris, who was Congress's virtual wartime economic czar, got Congress to charter the first Central Bank, his own Bank of North America (BNA). Like the Bank of England, Congress bestowed on Morris's private BNA the monopoly privilege of issuing paper notes throughout the country. Most of these notes were issued in the purchase of newly-issued federal debt, and the BNA was made the depository of all congressional funds. Over half the capital of the BNA was officially subscribed by Congress.[13] The BNA notes were supposedly redeemable in specie, but of course the fractional-reserve expansion indulged in by the BNA led to the depreciation of its notes outside its home base in Philadelphia. After the end of the Revolutionary War, Morris lost his national political power, and he was forced to privatize the BNA swiftly and to shift it to the status of a regular private bank shorn of government privilege.

Throughout the first century of the Republic, the party favoring a Central Bank, first the Hamiltonian High Federalists, then the Whigs and then the Republicans, was the party of Big Central Government, of a large public debt, of high

---

[13]When Morris failed to raise the specie capital legally required to launch the BNA, he simply appropriated specie loaned to the U.S. Treasury by France and invested it for the U.S. government in his own bank. On this episode, and on the history of the war over a Central Bank in America from then through the nineteenth century, see "The Minority Report of the U.S. Gold Commission of 1981," in the latest edition, *The Ron Paul Money Book* (Clute, Texas: Plantation Publishing, 1991), pp. 44–136.

protective tariffs, of large-scale public works, and of subsidies to large businesses in that early version of "partnership between government and industry." Protective tariffs were to subsidize domestic manufactures, while paper money, fractional reserve banking, and Central Banking were all advocated by the nationalists as part of a comprehensive policy of inflation and cheap credit in order to benefit favored businesses. These favorites were firms and industries that were part of the financial elite, centered from the beginning through the Civil War in Philadelphia and New York, with New York assuming first place after the end of that war.

Ranged against this powerful group of nationalists was an equally powerful movement dedicated to laissez-faire, free markets, free trade, ultra-minimal and decentralized government, and, in the monetary sphere, a hard-money system based squarely on gold and silver, with banks shorn of all special privileges and hopefully confined to 100-percent specie banking. These hard-money libertarians made up the heart and soul of the Jeffersonian Democratic-Republican and then the Jacksonian Democratic party, and their potential constituents permeated every occupation except those of banker and the banker's favored elite clientele.

After the First Bank of the United States was established by Hamilton, followed by a Second Bank put in by pro-bank Democrat-Republicans after the War of 1812, President Andrew Jackson managed to eliminate the Central Bank after a titanic struggle waged during the 1830s. While the Jacksonian Democrats were not able to enact their entire hard-money program during the 1840s and 1850s because of the growing Democratic split over slavery, the regime of those decades, in addition to establishing free trade for the last time in the United States, also managed to eliminate not only the Central Bank but all traces of centralized banking.

While the new Republican Party of the 1850s contained many former Jacksonian Democrats, the economic agenda of the Republicans was firmly fixed by the former Whigs in the party. The victorious Republicans took advantage of the near one-party Congress after the secession of the South to drive through their cherished agenda of economic nationalism and statism. This nationalist program included: a huge increase in central government power fueled by the first income tax and by heavy taxes on liquor and tobacco, vast land grants as well as monetary subsidies to new transcontinental railroads; and the reestablishment of a protective tariff.

Not the least of the Republican statist revolution was effected on the monetary and financial front. To finance the war effort against the South, the federal government went off the gold standard and issued irredeemable fiat paper money, called "Greenbacks" (technically, U.S. Notes). When the irredeemable paper, after two years, sank to 50 cents on the dollar on the market in terms of gold, the federal government turned increasingly to issuing public debt to finance the war.

Thus, the Republican-Whig program managed to dump the traditional Jefferson-Jackson Democratic devotion to hard money and gold, as well as their hatred of the public debt. (Both Jefferson, and later Jackson, in their administrations, managed, for the last time in American history, *to pay off* the federal public debt!) In addition, while the Republicans did not yet feel strong enough to bring back a Central Bank, they effectively put an end to the relatively free and non-inflationary banking system of the post-Jacksonian era, and created a new National Banking System that centralized the nation's banks, and established what amounted to a halfway house toward Central Banking.

The state banks had been happy, from the beginning of the war, to pyramid an expansion of fractional-reserve notes and demand deposits on top of the increase of federal greenbacks, thus expanding the total supply of money. Later in the Civil War, the federal government created the National Banking System, in the Bank Acts of 1863, 1864, and 1865. Whereas the Peel Act had granted to one Bank of England the monopoly of all bank notes, the National Banking Acts granted such a monopoly to a new category of federally chartered "national banks"; the existing state banks were prohibited from any issue of notes, and had to be confined to issuing bank deposits.[14] In other words, to obtain cash, or paper notes, the state banks had to keep their own deposit accounts at the national banks, so as to draw down their accounts and obtain cash to redeem their customers' deposits if necessary. For their part, the national banks were established in a centralized tripartite hierarchy. At the top of the hierarchy were leading "central reserve city" banks, a category originally confined to large banks in New York City; beneath that were "reserve city" banks, in cities of over 500,000 population; and beneath those were the rest, or "country banks." The new legislation featured a device pioneered by Whig

---

[14]Strictly, this prohibition was accomplished by a prohibitive 10-percent tax on state bank notes, levied by Congress in the spring of 1865 when the state banks disappointed Republican hopes by failing to rush to join the National Banking structure as set up in the two previous years.

state governments, especially New York and Michigan, in the 1840s: legal minimum fractional-reserve requirements of bank reserves to their notes and deposits. The reserve requirements fashioned an instrument of control by the upper strata of the banking hierarchy over the lower. The crucial point was to induce the lower tiers of banks to keep much of their reserves, not in legal cash (gold, silver, or greenbacks) but in demand deposit accounts in the higher tier banks.

Thus, the country banks had to keep a minimum ratio of 15 percent of reserves to their notes and demand deposits outstanding. Of that 15 percent, only 40 percent had to be in cash; the rest could be in the form of demand deposits at either reserve city or central reserve city banks. For their part, the reserve city banks, with a minimum reserve ratio of 25 percent, could keep no more than half of these reserves in cash; the other half could be kept as demand deposits in central reserve city banks, which also had to keep a minimum reserve ratio of 25 percent. These various national banks were to be chartered by a federal comptroller of the currency, an official of the Treasury Department. To obtain a charter, a bank had to obey high minimum capital requirements, requirements rising through the hierarchical categories of banks. Thus, the country banks needed to put up at least $50,000 in capital, and the reserve city banks faced a capital requirement of $200,000.

Before the Civil War, each state bank could only pyramid notes and deposits upon its own stock of gold and silver, and any undue expansion could easily bring it down from the redemption demands of other banks or the public. Each bank had to subsist on its own bottom. Moreover, any bank suspected of not being able to redeem its warehouse receipts, found its notes depreciating on the market compared either to gold or to the notes of other, sounder banks.

After the installation of the National Banking System, however, each bank was conspicuously *not* forced to stand on its own and be responsible for its own debts. The U. S. Government had now fashioned a hierarchical structure of four inverse pyramids, each inverse pyramid resting on top of a smaller, narrower one. At the bottom of this multi-tiered inverse pyramid were a handful of very large, central reserve city, Wall Street banks. On top of their reserves of gold, silver, and greenbacks, the Wall Street Banks could pyramid an expansion of notes and deposits by 4:1. On their deposits at the Central Reserve City banks, the reserve city banks could pyramid by 4:1, and then the country banks could pyramid their warehouse receipts by 6.67:1 on top of their deposits at the reserve banks. Finally, the state banks, forced to keep deposits at national banks, could pyramid *their* expansion of money and credit on top of their deposit accounts at the country or reserve city banks.

To eliminate the restriction on bank credit expansion of the depreciation of notes on the market, the Congress required all the national banks to accept each other's notes at par. The federal government conferred quasi-legal tender status on each national bank note by agreeing to accept them at par in taxes, and branch banking continued to be illegal as before the Civil War, so that a bank was only required to redeem notes in specie at the counter at its home office. In addition, the federal government made redemption in specie difficult by imposing a $3 million per month maximum limit on the contraction (i.e., net redemption) of national bank notes.

Thus, the country was saddled with a new, centralized, and far more unsound and inflationary banking system that could and did inflate on top of expansion by Wall Street banks. By being at the bottom of that pyramid, Wall Street banks could control as well as generate a multiple expansion of the nation's money and credit. Under cover of a "wartime emergency," the Republican Party had permanently transformed the nation's banking system from a fairly sound and decentralized one into an inflationary system under central Wall Street control.

The Democrats in Congress, devoted to hard money, had opposed the National Banking System almost to a man. It took the Democrats about a decade to recover politically from the Civil War, and their monetary energies were devoted during this period to end greenback inflationism and return to the gold standard, a victory which came in 1879 and which the Republicans resisted strongly. Particularly active in pushing for continued greenback inflation were the industrial and financial power elite among the Radical Republicans: the iron and steel industrialists and the big railroads. It was really the collapse of nationalist bankers, tycoons, and subsidized and over-expanded railroads in the mighty Panic of 1873 that humbled their political and economic power and permitted the victory of gold. The Panic was the consequence of the wartime and post-war inflationary boom generated by the new Banking System. And such dominant financial powers as Jay Cooke, the monopoly underwriter of government bonds from the Civil War on, and the main architect of the

National Banking System, was, in a fit of poetic justice, driven into bankruptcy by the Panic. But even after 1879, gold was still challenged by inflationist attempts to bring back or add silver to the monetary standard, and it took until 1900 before the silver threat was finally beaten back and gold established as the single monetary standard. Unfortunately, by that time, the Democrats had lost their status as a hard-money party, and were becoming more inflationist than the Republicans. In the midst of these struggles over the basic monetary standard, the dwindling stock of hard-money Democrats had neither the ability nor the inclination to try to restore the free and decentralized banking structure as it had existed before the Civil War.

Origins of the Federal Reserve: Wall Street Discontent

By the 1890s, the leading Wall Street bankers were becoming increasingly disgruntled with their own creation, the National Banking System. In the first place, while the banking system was partially centralized under their leadership, it was not centralized *enough*. Above all, there was no revered Central Bank to bail out the commercial banks when they got into trouble, to serve as a "lender of last resort." The big bankers couched their complaint in terms of "inelasticity." The money supply, they grumbled, wasn't "elastic" enough. In plain English, it couldn't be *increased* fast enough to suit the banks.

Specifically, the Wall Street banks found the money supply sufficiently "elastic" when they generated inflationary booms by means of credit expansion. The central reserve city banks could pyramid notes and deposits on top of gold, and thereby generate multiple inverse pyramids of monetary expansion on top of their own expansion of credit. That was fine. The problem came when, late in the inflationary booms, the banking system ran into trouble, and people started calling on the banks to redeem their notes and deposits in specie. At that point, since all of the banks were inherently insolvent, they, led by the Wall Street banks, were forced to contract their loans rapidly in order to stay in business, thereby causing a financial crisis and a system-wide contraction of the supply of money and credit. The banks were not interested in the contention that this sudden bust was a payback for, a wiping out of the excesses of, the inflationary boom that they had generated. They wanted to be able to keep expanding credit during recession as well as booms. Hence their call for a remedy to monetary "inelasticity" during recessions. And that remedy, of course, was the grand old nostrum that nationalists and bankers had been pushing for since the beginning of the Republic: a Central Bank.

Inelasticity was scarcely the only reason for the discontent of the Wall Street bankers with the *status quo*. Wall Street was also increasingly losing its dominance over the banking system. Originally, the Wall Street bankers thought that the state banks would be eliminated completely because of the prohibition on their issue of notes; instead, the state banks recouped by shifting to the issue of demand deposits and pyramiding on top of national bank issues. But far worse: the state banks and other private banks began to outcompete the national banks for financial business. Thus, while national banks were totally dominant immediately after the Civil War, by 1896 state banks, savings banks, and private banks comprised a full 54 percent of all bank resources. The relative growth of the state banks at the expense of the nationals was the result of National Bank Act regulations: for example, the high capital requirements for national banks, and the fact that national banks were prohibited from having a savings department, or from extending mortgage credit on real estate. Moreover, by the turn of the twentieth century, state banks had become dominant in the growing trust business.

Not only that: even within the national banking structure, New York was losing its predominance vis-à-vis banks in other cities. At the outset, New York City was the only central reserve city in the nation. In 1887, however, Congress amended the National Banking Act to allow cities with a population over 200,000 to become central reserve cities, and Chicago and St. Louis immediately qualified. These cities were indeed growing much faster than New York. As a result, Chicago and St. Louis, which had 16 percent of total Chicago, St. Louis, and New York bank deposits in 1880 were able to double their proportion of the three cities' deposits to 33 percent by 1910.[15]

In short, it was time for the Wall Street bankers to revive the idea of a Central Bank, and to impose full centralization with themselves in control: a lender of last resort that would place the prestige and resources of the federal government on the line in behalf of fractional-reserve banking. It was time to bring to America the post-Peel Act Central Bank.

---

[15]See Gabriel Kolko, *The Triumph of Conservatism: A Reinterpretation of American History, 1890–1916* (New York: Free Press, 1963), pp. 140–42.

The first task, however, was to beat down the Populist insurrection, which, with the charismatic pietist William Jennings Bryan at its head, was considered a grave danger by the Wall Street bankers. For two reasons: one, the Populists were much more frankly inflationist than the bankers; and two and more importantly, they distrusted Wall Street and wanted an inflation which would sidestep the banks and be outside banker control. Their particular proposal was an inflation brought about by monetizing silver, stressing the more abundant silver rather than the scarcer metal gold as the key means of inflating the money supply.

Bryan and his populists had taken control of the Democratic Party, previously a hard-money party, at its 1896 national convention, and thereby transformed American politics. Led by the most powerful investment banker, Wall Street's J. P. Morgan & Company, all the nation's financial groups worked together to defeat the Bryanite menace, aiding McKinley to defeat Bryan in 1896, and then cemented the victory in McKinley's reelection in 1900. In that way, they were able to secure the Gold Standard Act of 1900, ending the silver threat once and for all. It was then time to move on to the next task: a Central Bank for the United States.

Putting Cartelization
Across: The Progressive Line

The origin of the Federal Reserve has been deliberately shrouded in myth spread by pro-Fed apologists. The official legend holds that the idea of a Central Bank in America originated after the Panic of 1907, when the banks, stung by the financial panic, concluded that drastic reform, highlighted by the establishment of a lender of last resort, was desperately necessary.

All this is rubbish. The Panic of 1907 provided a convenient handle to stir up the public and spread pro-Central Bank propaganda. In actuality, the banker agitation for a Central Bank began as soon as the 1896 McKinley victory over Bryan was secured.

The second crucial part of the official legend claims that a Central Bank is necessary to curb the commercial banks' unfortunate tendency to over-expand, such booms giving rise to subsequent busts. An "impartial" Central Bank, on the other hand, driven as it is by the public interest, could and would restrain the banks from their natural narrow and selfish tendency to make profits at the expense of the public weal. The stark fact that it was bankers themselves who were making this argument was supposed to attest to their nobility and altruism.

In fact, as we have seen, the banks desperately desired a Central Bank, not to place fetters on their own natural tendency to inflate, but, on the contrary, to enable them to inflate and expand together without incurring the penalties of market competition. As a lender of last resort, the Central Bank could permit and encourage them to inflate when they would ordinarily have to contract their loans in order to save themselves. In short, the real reason for the adoption of the Federal Reserve, and its promotion by the large banks, was the exact opposite of their loudly trumpeted motivations. Rather than create an institution to curb their own profits on behalf of the public interest, the banks sought a Central Bank to enhance their profits by permitting them to inflate far beyond the bounds set by free-market competition.

The bankers, however, faced a big public relations problem. What they wanted was the federal government creating and enforcing a banking cartel by means of a Central Bank. Yet they faced a political climate that was hostile to monopoly and centralization, and favored free competition. They also faced a public opinion hostile to Wall Street and to what they perceptively but inchoately saw as the "money power." The bankers also confronted a nation with a long tradition of opposing Central Banking. How then, could they put a Central Bank across?

It is important to realize that the problem faced by the big bankers was only one facet of a larger problem. Finance capital, led once again and not coincidentally by the Morgan Bank, had been trying without success to cartelize the economy on the free market. First, in the 1860s and 1870s, the Morgans, as the major financiers and underwriters of America's first big business, the railroads; tried desperately and repeatedly to cartelize railroads: to arrange railroad "pools" to restrict shipments, allocate shipments among themselves, and raise freight rates, in order to increase profits in the railroad industry. Despite the Morgan clout and a ready willingness by most of the railroad magnates, the attempts kept floundering, shattered on the rock of market competition, as individual railroads cheated on the agreement in order to pick up quick profits, and new venture capital built competing railroads to take advantage of the high cartel prices. Finally, the Morgan-led railroads turned to the federal government to regulate railroads and thereby to enforce the cartel that they could not achieve on the free market. Hence the Interstate Commerce Commission, established in 1887.[16]

In general, manufacturing firms did not become large enough to incorporate until the 1890s, and at that point the investment bankers financing the corporations, again led by the Morgans, organized a large series of giant mergers, covering literally hundreds of industries. Mergers would avoid the problem of cheating by separate individual firms, and monopoly firms could then proceed peacefully to restrict production, raise prices, and increase profits for all the merged firms and stockholders. The mighty merger movement peaked from 1898–1902. Unfortunately, once again, virtually all of these mergers flopped badly, failing to establish monopolies or monopoly prices, and in some cases steadily losing market shares from then on and even plunging into bankruptcy. Again the problem was new venture capital entering the industry and, armed with up-to-date equipment, outcompeting the cartel at the artificially high price. And once again, the Morgan financial interests, joined by other financial and big business groups, decided that they needed the government, in particular the federal government, to be their surrogate in establishing and, better yet, enforcing the cartel.[17]

[16]See Gabriel Kolko, *Railroads and Regulation, 1877–1916* (Princeton: Princeton University Press, 1965).

[17]See Kolko, *Triumph of Conservatism*, pp. 1–56; Naomi Lamoureaux, *The Great Merger Movement in American Business, 1895–104* (New York: Cambridge University Press,1985); Arthur S. Dewing, *Corporate Promotions and Reorganizations* (Cambridge, Mass.: Harvard University Press, 1914); and *idem, The Financial Policy of Corporations*, 2 vols., 5th ed. (New York: Ronald Press, 1953).

The famed Progressive Era, an era of a Great Leap Forward in massive regulation of business by state and federal government, stretched approximately from 1900 or the late 1890s through World War I. The Progressive Era was essentially put through by the Morgans and their allies in order to cartelize American business and industry, to take up more effectively where the cartel and merger movements had left off. It should be clear that the Federal Reserve System, established in 1913, was part and parcel of that Progressive movement: just as the large meat packers managed to put through costly federal inspection of meat in 1906, in order to place cripplingly high costs on competing small meat packers, so the big bankers cartelized banking through the Federal Reserve System seven years later.[18]

Just as the big bankers, in trying to set up a Central Bank, had to face a public opinion suspicious of Wall Street and hostile to Central Banking, so the financiers and industrialists faced a public steeped in a tradition and ideology of free competition and hostility to monopoly. How could they get the public and legislators to go along with the fundamental transformation of the American economy toward cartels and monopoly?

The answer was the same in both cases: the big businessmen and financiers had to form an alliance with the opinion-molding classes in society, in order to engineer the consent of the public by means of crafty and persuasive propaganda. The opinion-molding classes, in previous centuries the Church, but now consisting of media people, journalists,

---

[18]On meatpacking, see Kolko, *Triumph of Conservatism*, pp. 98–108.

intellectuals, economists and other academics, professionals, educators as well as ministers, had to be enlisted in this cause. For their part the intellectuals and opinion-molders were all too ready for such an alliance. In the first place, most of the academics, economists, historians, social scientists, had gone to Germany in the late nineteenth century to earn their Ph.D.s, which were not yet being granted widely in the U.S. There they had become imbued with the ideals of Bismarckian statism, organicism, collectivism, and State molding and governing of society, with bureaucrats and other planners benignly ruling over a cartelized economy in partnership with organized big business.

There was also a more direct economic reason for the intellectuals' eagerness for this new statist coalition. The late nineteenth century had seen an enormous expansion and professionalization of the various segments of intellectuals and technocrats. Suddenly, tool-and-die men had become graduate engineers; gentlemen with bachelor's degrees had proliferated into specialized doctorates; physicians, social workers, psychiatrists, all these groups had formed themselves into guilding and professional associations. What they wanted from the State was plush and prestigious jobs and grants (a) to help run and plan the new statist system; and (b) to apologize for the new order. These guilds were also anxious to have the State license or otherwise restrict entry into their professions and occupations, in order to raise the incomes of each guildsman.

Hence the new alliance of State and Opinion-Molder, an old-fashioned union of Throne and Altar recycled and updated into a partnership of government, business leader, intellectual, and expert. During the Progressive Era, by far the most important forum established by Big Business and Finance which drew together all the leaders of these groups, hammered out a common ideology and policy program, and actually drafted and lobbied for the leading new Progressive measures of state and federal intervention, was the National Civic Federation; other similar and more specialized groups followed.[19]

It was not enough, however, for the new statist alliance of Big Business and Big Intellectuals to be formed; they had to agree, propound, and push for a common ideological line, a line that would persuade the majority of the public to adopt the new program and even greet it with enthusiasm. The new line was brilliantly successful if deceptive: that the new Progressive measures and regulations were necessary to save the public interest from sinister and exploitative Big Business monopoly, which business was achieving on the free market. Government policy, led by intellectuals, academics and disinterested experts in behalf of the public weal, was to "save" capitalism, and correct the faults and failures of the free market by establishing government control and planning in the public interest. In other words, policies, such as the Interstate Commerce Act, drafted and operated to try to enforce railroad cartels, were to be advocated in terms of bringing the Big Bad Railroads to heel by means of democratic government action.

[19]On the National Civic Federation, see James Weinstein, *The Corporate Ideal in the Liberal State, 1890–1918* (Boston: Beacon Press, 1968). Also see David Eakins, "The Development of Corporate Liberal Policy Research in the United States 1885–1965" (doctoral dissertation, Department of History, University of Wisconsin, 1966).

Throughout this successful "corporate liberal" imposture, beginning in the Progressive Era and continuing ever since, one glaring public relations problem has confronted this big business-intellectual coalition. If these policies are designed to tame and curb rapacious Big Business, how is it that so many Big Businessmen, so many Morgan partners and Rockefellers and Harrimans, have been so conspicuous in promoting these programs? The answer, though seemingly naive, has managed to persuade the public with little difficulty: that these men are Enlightened, educated, public-spirited businessmen, filled with the aristocratic spirit of *noblesse oblige*, whose seemingly quasi-suicidal activities and programs are performed in the noble spirit of sacrifice for the good of humanity. Educated in the spirit of service, they have been able to rise above the mere narrow and selfish grasp for profit that had marked their own forefathers.

And then, should any maverick skeptic arise, who refuses to fall for this hokum and tries to dig more deeply into the economic motivations at work, he will be quickly and brusquely dismissed as an "extremist" (whether of Left or Right), a malcontent, and, most damning of all, a "believer in the conspiracy theory of history." The question here, however, is not some sort of "theory of history," but a willingness to use one's common sense. All that the analyst or historian need do is to assume, as an hypothesis, that people in government or lobbying for government policies may be *at least* as self-interested and profit-motivated as people in business or everyday life, and then to investigate the significant and revealing patterns that he will see before his eyes.

Central Banking, in short, was designed to "do for" the banks what the ICC had "done for" the railroads, the Meat Inspection Act had done for the big meatpackers, etc. In the case of Central Banking, the Line that had to be pushed was a variant of the "anti-Big Business" shell game being perpetrated on behalf of Big Business throughout the Progressive Era. In banking, the line was that a Central Bank was necessary to curb the inflationary excesses of unregulated banks on the free market. And if Big Bankers were rather conspicuous and early in advocating such a measure, why this only showed that they were more educated, more Enlightened, and more nobly public-spirited than the rest of their banking brethren.

Putting a Central Bank Across: Manipulating a Movement, 1897–1902

Around 1900, two mighty financial–industrial groups, each consisting of investment banks, commercial banks, and industrial resources, confronted each other, usually with hostility, in the financial, and more importantly, the political arena. These coalitions were (1) the interests grouped around the Morgan bank; and (2) an alliance of Rockefeller–Harriman and Kuhn, Loeb interests. It became far easier for these financial elites to influence and control politicians and political affairs after 1900 than before. For the "Third Party System," which had existed in America from 1856 to 1896, was comprised of political parties, each of which was highly ideological and in intense conflict with the opposing party. While each political party, in this case the Democratic, the Republican, and various minor parties, consisted of a coalition of interests and forces, each was dominated by a firm ideology to which it was strongly committed. As a result, citizens often felt lifelong party loyalties, were socialized into a party when growing up, were educated in party principles, and then rode herd on any party candidates who waffled or betrayed the cause. For various reasons, the Democratic and Republican parties after 1900, in the Fourth and later Party Systems, were largely non-ideological, differed very little from each other, and as a result commanded little party loyalty. In particular, the Democratic Party no longer existed, after the Bryan takeover of 1896, as a committed laissez-faire, hard-money party. From then on, both parties rapidly became Progressive and moderately statist.[20]

Since the importance of political parties dwindled after 1900, and ideological laissez-faire restraints on government intervention were gravely weakened, the power of financiers in government increased markedly. Furthermore, Congress—the arena of political parties—became less important. A power vacuum developed for the intellectuals and technocratic experts to fill the executive bureaucracy, and to run and plan national economic life relatively unchecked.

The House of Morgan had begun, in the 1860s and 70s, as an investment bank financing and controlling railroads, and then, in later decades, moved into manufacturing and commercial banking. In the opposing coalition, the Rockefellers had begun in oil and moved into commercial banking; Harriman had earned his spurs as a brilliant railroad investor and entrepreneur in competition with the Morgans; and

---

[20]See, among others, Paul Kleppner, *The Third Electoral System, 1853–1892: Parties, Voters, and Political Cultures* (Chapel Hill: University of North Carolina Press, 1979).

Kuhn, Loeb began in investment banking financing manufacturing. From the 1890s until World War II, much of American political history, of programs and conflicts, can be interpreted not so much as "Democrat" versus "Republican," but as the interaction or conflict between the Morgans and their allies on the one hand, and the Rockefeller–Harriman-Kuhn, Loeb alliance on the other.

Thus, Grover Cleveland spent his working life allied with the Morgans, and his cabinet and policies were heavily Morgan-oriented; William McKinley, on the other hand, a Republican from Rockefeller's home state of Ohio, was completely in the Rockefeller camp. In contrast, McKinley's vice-president, who suddenly assumed the presidency when McKinley was assassinated, was Theodore Roosevelt, whose entire life was spent in the Morgan ambit. When Roosevelt suddenly trotted out the Sherman Antitrust Act, previously a dead letter, to try to destroy Rockefeller's Standard Oil as well as Harriman's control of the Northern Pacific Railroad, this led to a titanic struggle between the two mighty financial groups. President Taft, an Ohio Republican who was close to the Rockefellers, struck back by trying to destroy the two main Morgan trusts, United States Steel and International Harvester. Infuriated, the Morgans created the new Progressive Party in 1912, headed by Morgan partner George W. Perkins, and induced the popular ex-President Roosevelt to run for a third term on the Progressive ticket. The aim, and the result, was to destroy Taft's chances for re-election, and to elect the first Democratic president in twenty years, Woodrow Wilson.[21]

---

[21]Thus, see Philip H. Burch, Jr., *Elites in American History, Vol. 2: From the Civil War to the New Deal* (New York: Holmes & Meier, 1981).

But while the two financial groups clashed on many issues and personalities, on some matters they agreed and were able to work in concert. Thus, both groups favored the new trend toward cartelization in the name of Progressivism and curbing alleged Big Business monopoly, and both groups, led by the Morgans, were happy to collaborate in the National Civic Federation.

On banking and on the alleged necessity for a central bank, both groups, again, were in happy agreement. And while later on in the history of the Federal Reserve there would be a mighty struggle for control between the factions, to found the Fed they were able to work in undisturbed harmony, and even tacitly agreed that the Morgan Bank would take the lead and play the role of first among equals.[22]

The bank reform movement, sponsored by the Morgan and Rockefeller forces, began as soon as the election of McKinley as President in 1896 was secured, and the populist Bryan menace beaten back. The reformers decided not to shock people by calling for a central bank right away, but to move toward it slowly, first raising the general point that the money supply must be cured of its "inelasticity." The bankers decided to employ the techniques they had used successfully

---

[22]J. P. Morgan's fondness for a central bank was heightened by the memory of the fact that the bank of which his father Junius was junior partner—the London firm of George Peabody and Company—was saved from bankruptcy in the Panic of 1857 by an emergency credit from the Bank of England. The elder Morgan took over the firm upon Peabody's retirement, and its name was changed to J. S. Morgan and Company. See Ron Chernow, *The House of Morgan* (New York: Atlantic Monthly Press, 1990), pp. 11–12.

in generating a mass pro–gold standard movement in 1895 and 1896. The crucial point was to avoid the damaging appearance of Wall Street prominence and control in the new movement, by creating a spurious "grass roots" movement of non-banker businessmen, centered in the noble American heartland of the Middle West, far from the sinful environs of Wall Street. It was important for bankers, *a fortiori* Wall Street bankers, to take a discreet back seat in the reform movement, which was to consist seemingly of heartland businessmen, academics, and other supposedly disinterested experts.

The reform movement was officially launched just after the 1896 election by Hugh Henry Hanna, president of the Atlas Engine Works of Indianapolis, who had been active in the gold standard movement earlier in the year; Hanna sent a memorandum to the Indianapolis Board of Trade urging a heartland state like Indiana to take the lead in currency reform.[23] The reformers responded with remarkable speed. Answering the call of the Indianapolis Board of Trade, delegates of Boards of Trade from twelve midwestern cities met in Indianapolis at the beginning of December, and they called for a large monetary convention of businessmen from 26 states, which met quickly in Indianapolis on January 12. This Indianapolis Monetary Convention (IMC) resolved: (a) to urge President McKinley to continue the gold standard; and (b) to urge the president to create a new system of "elastic" bank credit, by appointing a Monetary

---

[23]For the memorandum, see by far the best book on the movement culminating in the Federal Reserve System, James Livingston, *Origins of the Federal Reserve System: Money, Class, and Corporate Capitalism, 1890–1913* (Ithaca, N.Y.: Cornell University Press, 1986).

Commission to prepare legislation for a revised monetary system. The IMC named Hugh Hanna as chairman of a permanent executive committee that he would appoint to carry out these policies.

The influential *Yale Review* hailed the IMC for deflecting opposition by putting itself forward as a gathering of businessmen rather than bankers. But to those in the know, it was clear that the leading members of the executive committee were important financiers in the Morgan ambit. Two particularly powerful executive members were Alexander E. Orr, Morgan-oriented New York City banker, grain merchandiser, railroad director, and director of the J. P. Morgan-owned publishing house of Harper Brothers; and Milwaukee tycoon Henry C. Payne, a Republican leader, head of the Morgan-dominated Wisconsin Telephone Company, and long-time director of the North American Company, a giant public utility holding company. So close was North American to the Morgan interests that its board included two top Morgan financiers; Edmund C. Converse, president of the Morgan-run Liberty National Bank of New York, and soon to be founding president of Morgan's Bankers Trust Company; and Robert Bacon, a partner in J. P. Morgan & Company, and one of Theodore Roosevelt's closest friends.[24]

A third member of the IMC executive committee was an even more powerful secretary of the committee and was even closer to the Morgan empire. He was George Hoster Peabody. The entire Peabody family of Boston Brahmins

[24]When Theodore Roosevelt became president he made Bacon Assistant Secretary of State, while Henry Payne took the top political job of Postmaster General of the United States.

had long been personally and financially closely associated with the Morgans. A George Peabody had established an international banking firm of which J. P. Morgan's father, Junius, had been a senior partner. A member of the Peabody clan had served as best man at J. P. Morgan's wedding in 1865. George Foster Peabody was an eminent, politically left-liberal, New York investment banker, who was to help the Morgans reorganize one of their prime industrial firms, General Electric, and who was later offered the job of Secretary of Treasury in the Wilson Administration. Although he turned down the official post, Peabody functioned throughout the Wilson regime as a close adviser and "statesman without portfolio."

President McKinley was highly favorable to the IMC, and in his First Inaugural Address, he endorsed the idea of "some revision" of the banking system. He followed this up in late July, 1897 with a special message to Congress, proposing the establishment of a special monetary commission. A bill for a commission passed the House, but failed in the Senate.

Disappointed but imperturbable, the executive committee of the IMC decided in August to select their own Indianapolis Monetary Commission. The leading role in appointing the new Commission was played by George Foster Peabody. The Commission consisted of various industrial notables, almost all either connected with Morgan railroads or, in one case, with the Morgan-controlled General Electric Company.[25] The

[25]Some examples: Former Secretary of the Treasury (under Cleveland) Charles S. Fairchild, a leading New York banker, former partner in the Boston Brahmin, Morgan-oriented investment banking firm of Lee, Higginson & Company. Fairchild's father, Sidney T., had been a leading

working head of the Monetary Commission was economist J. Laurence Laughlin, head Professor of Political Economy at the University of Chicago, and editor of the university's prestigious *Journal of Political Economy*. Laughlin supervised the operations of the Commission staff and the writings of its reports; the staff consisted of two of Laughlin's graduate students at Chicago.

The then impressive sum of $50,000 was raised throughout the nation's banking and corporate community to finance the work of the Indianapolis Monetary Commission. New York City's large quota was raised by Morgan bankers Peabody and Orr, and a large contribution came from none other than J. P. Morgan himself.

Setting up shop in Washington in mid-September, the Commission staff pioneered in persuasive public relations techniques to spread the reports of the Commission far and wide. In the first place, they sent a detailed monetary questionnaire to several hundred selected "impartial" experts, who they were sure would answer the questions in the desired manner. These questionnaire answers were then trumpeted as the received opinions of the nation's business community. Chairman of the IMC Hugh Hanna

---

attorney for the Morgan-controlled New York Central Railroad. Another member of the Commission was Stuyvesant Fish, scion of two long-time aristocratic New York families, partner of the Morgan-dominated New York investment bank of Morton, Bliss & Company, and president of the Illinois Central Railroad. A third member was William B. Dean, merchant from St. Paul, Minnesota, and a director of the St. Paul-based transcontinental railroad, Great Northern, owned by James J. Hill, a powerful ally of Morgan in his titanic battle with Harriman, Rockefeller, and Kuhn, Loeb for control of the Northern Pacific Railroad.

made the inspired choice of hiring as Washington assistant of the Commission the financial journalist Charles A. Conant, who had recently written *A History of Modern Banks of Issue*. The Monetary Commission was due to issue its preliminary report in mid-December; by early December, Conant was beating the drums for the Commission's recommendations, leading an advance line of the report in an issue of *Sound Currency* magazine, and bolstering the Commission's proposals with frequent reports of unpublished replies to the Commission's questionnaire. Conant and his colleagues induced newspapers throughout the country to print abstracts of these questionnaire answers, and in that way, as the Commission's secretary reported, by "careful manipulation" were able to get part or all of the preliminary Commission report printed in nearly 7,500 newspapers, large and small, across the nation. Thus, long before the days of computerized direct mail, Conant and the others on the staff developed a distribution or transmission system of nearly 100,000 correspondents "dedicated to the enactment of the commission's plan for banking and currency reform."[26]

The prime emphasis of the Commission's preliminary report was to complete the McKinley victory by codifying the existing *de facto* single gold standard. More important in the long run was a call for fundamental banking reform to allow greater "elasticity," so that bank credit could be increased during recessions. As yet, there were little specifics for such a long-run transformation.

[26]Livingston, *Origins*, pp. 109–10.

The executive committee now decided to organize the second and final meeting of the Indianapolis Monetary Convention, which met at that city in January, 1898. The second convention was a far grander affair than the first, bringing together nearly 500 delegates from 31 states. Moreover, the gathering was a cross-section of America's top corporate leaders. The purpose of this second convention, as former Secretary of the Treasury Fairchild candidly explained to the gathering, was to mobilize the nation's leading businessmen into a mighty and influential banking reform movement. As he put it, "If men of business give serious attention and study to these subjects, they will substantially agree upon legislation, and thus, agreeing, their influence will be prevailing." Presiding officer of the convention, Iowa's Governor Leslie M. Shaw, was, however, a bit disingenuous when he told the meeting: "You represent today not the banks, for there are few bankers on this floor. You represent the business industries and the financial interests of the country." For there were plenty of bankers there, too. Shaw himself, later to be Secretary of the Treasury under Theodore Roosevelt, was a small-town banker in Iowa, president of the Bank of Denison, who saw nothing wrong with continuing in this post throughout his term as governor. More important for Shaw's career was the fact that he was a long-time leading member of the Des Moines Regency, the Iowa Republican machine headed by powerful Senator William Boyd Allison. Allison, who was later to obtain the Treasury post for Shaw, was in turn closely tied to Charles E. Perkins, a close Morgan ally, president of the Chicago, Burlington and Quincy Railroad, and kinsman of the highly influential Forbes financial group of Boston, long tied to the Morgan interests.

Also serving as delegates to this convention were several eminent economists who, however, intriguingly came not as academic observers but frankly as representatives of sections of the business community. Thus Professor Jeremiah W. Jenks of Cornell, a leading proponent of government cartelization and enforcement of trusts and soon to become a friend and advisor of Theodore Roosevelt as governor of New York, came as a delegate from the Ithaca Business Men's Association. Frank W. Taussig of Harvard represented the Cambridge Merchant's Association; Yale's Arthur Twining Hadley, soon to become president of Yale University, came as representative of the New Haven Chamber of Commerce; and Fred M. Taylor of the University of Michigan came representing the Ann Arbor Business Men's Association. Each of these men held powerful posts in the organized economics profession, Jenks, Taussig, and Taylor serving on the Currency Committee of the American Economic Association. Hadley, a leading railroad economist, also served on the board of directors of two leading Morgan railroads: the New York, New Haven and Hartford, and the Atchison, Topeka, and Santa Fe Railroads.

Both Taussig and Taylor were monetary theorists who urged reform to make the money supply more elastic. Taussig wanted an expansion of national bank notes, to inflate in response to the "needs of business," so that the currency would "grow without trammels as the needs of the community spontaneously call for increase." Taylor, too, urged a modification of the gold standard by "a conscious control of the movement of money" by government "in order to maintain the stability of the credit system." Taylor went so far as to justify suspensions of specie payment by the government in order to "protect the gold reserve."[27]

In late January, the Convention duly endorsed the preliminary report with virtual unanimity, after which Professor Laughlin was assigned the task of drawing up a more elaborate Final Report of the Commission, which was published and distributed a few months later. With the endorsement of the august membership of the Convention secured, Laughlin's Final Report finally let the cat out of the bag: for the report not only came out for a greatly increased issue of national bank notes, but it also called explicitly for a Central Bank that would enjoy a monopoly of the issue of bank notes.[28]

The Convention delegates promptly took the gospel of banking reform and a central bank to the length and breadth of the corporate and financial communities. Thus, in April, 1898, A. Barton Hepburn, monetary historian and president of the Chase National Bank of New York, at that time the flagship commercial bank for the Morgan interests, and a man who would play a leading role in the drive to establish a central bank, invited Monetary Commissioner Robert S. Taylor to address the New York State Bankers' Association

[27]Joseph Dorfman, *The Economic Mind in American Civilization* (New York: Viking Press, 1949), vol. 3, pp. xxxviii, 269, 392–93.

[28]The Final Report, including the recommendation for a Central Bank, was hailed by Convention delegate F. M. Taylor in Laughlin's economic journal, the *Journal of Political Economy*. Taylor also exulted that the Convention had been "one of the most notable movements of our time— the first thoroughly organized movement of the business classes in the whole country directed to the bringing about of a radical change in national legislation." F. M. Taylor, "The Final Report to the Indianapolis Monetary Commission," *Journal of Political Economy* 6 (June 1898): 322.

on the currency question, since "bankers, like other people, need instruction on this subject." All the Monetary Commissioners, especially Taylor, were active during this period in exhorting groups of businessmen throughout the nation on behalf of banking reform.[29]

Meanwhile, the lobbying team of Hanna and Conant were extremely active in Washington. A bill embodying the proposals of the Indianapolis Monetary Commission was introduced into the House by Indiana Congressman Jesse Overstreet in January, and was reported out by the House Banking and Currency Committee in May. In the meanwhile, Conant met also continually with the Banking Committee members, while Hanna repeatedly sent circular letters to the Convention delegates and to the public, urging a letter-writing campaign in support of the bill at every step of the Congressional process.

Amidst this agitation, McKinley's Secretary of the Treasury, Lyman J. Gage, worked closely with Hanna, Conant, and their staff. Gage sponsored several bills along the same lines. Gage, a friend of several of the Monetary Commissioners, was one of the top leaders of the Rockefeller interests in the banking field. His appointment as Secretary of the Treasury had been secured for him by Ohio's Mark Hanna, political mastermind and financial backer of President McKinley, and old friend, high school classmate, and business associate of John D. Rockefeller, Sr. Before his appointment to the Cabinet, Gage had been president of the powerful First National Bank of Chicago, one of the leading commercial banks in the

[29]Taylor was an Indiana attorney for General Electric Company.

Rockefeller ambit. During his term in office, Gage tried to operate the Treasury Department as a central bank, pumping in money during recessions by purchasing government bonds in the open market, and depositing large funds with pet commercial banks.

In 1900, Gage called vainly for the establishment of regional central banks. Finally, in his last annual report as Secretary of the Treasury in 1901, Lyman Gage called outright for a governmental central bank. Without such a central bank, he declared in alarm, "individual banks stand isolated and apart, separated units, with no tie of mutuality between them." Unless a central bank could establish such ties, he warned, the Panic of 1893 would be repeated.

Any reform legislation, however, had to wait until the gold forces could secure control of Congress in the elections of 1898. In the autumn, the permanent executive committee of the Indianapolis Monetary Convention mobilized its forces, calling on 97,000 correspondents throughout the country to whom it had distributed its preliminary report. The executive committee urged its readers to elect a gold standard Congress, a task which was accomplished in November.

As a result, the McKinley Administration now could submit its bill to codify the single gold standard, which Congress passed as the Gold Standard Act of March, 1900. Phase One of the reformers' task had been accomplished: gold was the sole standard, and the silver menace had been crushed. Less well-known are the clauses of the Gold Standard Act that began the march toward a more "elastic" currency. Capital requirements for national banks in small towns and rural areas were now loosened, and it was made easier for national banks to issue notes. The purpose was to meet a popular demand for "more money" in rural areas at crop-moving time.

But the reformers regarded the Gold Standard Act as only the first step toward fundamental banking reform. Thus, Frank Taussig, in Harvard's economic journal, praised the Gold Standard Act, and was particularly gratified that it was the result of a new social and ideological alignment, sparked by "strong pressure from the business community" through the Indianapolis Monetary Convention. But Taussig warned that more reform was needed to allow for greater expansion of money and bank credit.[30]

More detailed in calling for reform in his comment on the Gold Standard Act was Joseph French Johnson, Professor of Finance at the Wharton School of Business at the University of Pennsylvania. Johnson deplored the U. S. banking system as the worst in the world, and pointed in contrast to the glorious central banking systems existing in Britain and France. In the United States, however, unfortunately "there is no single business institution, and no group of large institutions, in which self-interest, responsibility, and power naturally unite and conspire for the protection of the monetary system against twists and strains." In short, there was far too much freedom and decentralization in the banking system, so that the deposit credit structure "trembles" whenever credit expansion leads to demands for cash or gold.[31]

---

[30]Frank W. Taussig, "The Currency Act of 1900," *Quarterly Journal of Economics* 14 (May 1900): 415.

[31]Joseph French Johnson, "The Currency Act of March 14, 1900," *Political Science Quarterly* 15 (1900): 482–507.

Johnson had been a mentor and close friend at the *Chicago Tribune* of both Lyman Gage and Frank A. Vanderlip , who was to play a particularly important role in the drive for a central bank. When Gage went to Washington as Secretary of the Treasury, he brought Vanderlip along as his Assistant Secretary. On the accession of Roosevelt to the Presidency, Gage left the Cabinet in early 1902, and Gage, Vanderlip, and Conant all left for top banking positions in New York.[32]

The political pressure for reform after 1900 was poured on by the large bankers. A. Barton Hepburn, head of Morgan's Chase National Bank, drew up a bill as head of a commission of the American Bankers Association, and the bill was submitted to Congress in late 1901 by Representative Charles N. Fowler of New Jersey, chairman of the House Banking and Currency Committee. The Hepburn–Fowler Bill was reported out of the committee the following April. The Fowler Bill allowed for further expansion of national bank notes; it also allowed national banks to establish branches at home and abroad, a step that had been illegal (and has still been illegal until very recently) due to the fierce opposition of the small country bankers. Third, the Fowler Bill proposed to create a three-member board of control within the Treasury Department to supervise new bank notes and to establish clearinghouses. This would have been a step toward a central bank. But, at this point, fierce opposition by the country bankers managed to kill the Fowler Bill on the

[32]Gage became president of the Rockefeller-controlled U.S. Trust Company; Vanderlip became vice-president at the flagship commercial bank of the Rockefeller interests, the National City Bank of New York; and Conant became Treasurer of the Morgan-controlled Morton Trust Company.

floor of the House in 1902, despite agitation in its favor by the executive committee and staff of the Indianapolis Monetary Convention.

Thus, the opposition of the small country bankers managed to stop the reform drive in Congress. Trying another tack, Theodore Roosevelt's Secretary of Treasury Leslie Shaw attempted to continue and expand Lyman Gage's experiments in making the U.S. Treasury function like a central bank. In particular, Shaw made open-market purchases in recessions and violated the Independent Treasury statutes confining Treasury funds to its own vaults, by depositing Treasury funds in favored large national banks. In his last annual report of 1906, Secretary Shaw urged that he be given total power to regulate all the nation's banks. But by this time, the reformers had all dubbed these efforts a failure; a central bank itself was deemed clearly necessary.

The Central Bank Movement Revives, 1906–1910

After the failure of the first drive toward central banking with the defeat of the Fowler Bill in 1902, and the collapse of Secretary Shaw's efforts to use the Treasury as a surrogate central bank, the bank reform forces decided to put their cards on the table and push frankly for a Central Bank for the United States.

The revived campaign was kicked off by a fateful speech in January 1906 by the powerful Jacob H. Schiff, head of the Wall Street investment banking firm of Kuhn, Loeb & Company before the New York Chamber of Commerce. Schiff complained that the country had "needed money" in the autumn of 1905, and couldn't obtain it from the Treasury. An "elastic currency" for the nation was therefore imperative, and Schiff urged the New York Chamber's Committee on Finance to draw up a comprehensive plan for a new modern banking system to provide for a comprehensive plan for a new modern banking system to provide for an elastic currency. A Kuhn, Loeb partner and kinsman of Schiff who had agitated behind the scenes for a central bank was Paul Moritz Warburg, who had suggested the idea to Schiff as early as 1903. Warburg had emigrated in 1897 from the German investment banking firm of M. M. Warburg & Company and was devoted to the central banking model that had developed in Germany.

When the Finance Committee of the New York Chamber proved reluctant, Frank A. Vanderlip reported this unwelcome development to his boss, James Stillman, head of the National City Bank, and Stillman suggested that a new five-man special commission be set up by the New York Chamber to report on a plan for currency reform. The important thing was to secure a commission predisposed to be friendly, and Vanderlip managed to secure a commission totally loaded in favor of a central bank. This special commission of the New York Chamber consisted of Vanderlip, a Rockefeller man; Schiff's close friend Isidore Straus, a director of R. H. Macy & Company; two Morgan men: Dumont Clarke, president of the American Exchange National Bank and a personal adviser to J. P. Morgan, and our old friend Charles A. Conant, treasurer of Morton Trust Company. The fifth member was John Claflin, of H. B. Claflin & Company, a large wholesaling firm, who was a veteran of the Indianapolis Monetary Convention. Coming on board as secretary of the new currency commission was Vanderlip's friend Professor Joseph French Johnson, now of New York University.

The commission revived the old Indianapolis questionnaire technique: acquiring legitimacy by sending out a detailed questionnaire on currency to a number of financial leaders. While Johnson mailed and collated the questionnaires, Conant visited and interviewed the heads of the central banks of Europe.

The special commission delivered its "Currency Report" to the New York Chamber in October, 1906. To eliminate instability and the danger of an inelastic currency, the commission called for the creation of a "central bank of issue under the control of the government." The following January, Paul Warburg went public with his agitation for a central bank, publishing two articles on its behalf. The big bankers recognized, however, that ever since the defeat of the Fowler Bill, a prime task would be to convert the large number of small bankers in the nation to the cause of a central bank.

The Panic of 1907 struck in October, the result of an inflation stimulated by Secretary of the Treasury Leslie Shaw in the previous two years. The Panic galvanized the big bankers to put on a concerted *putsch* for a Lender of Last Resort in the shape of a central bank. The big bankers realized that one of the first steps in the march to a central bank was to win the support of the nation's economists, academics, and financial experts. Fortunately for the reformers, two useful organizations for the mobilization of academics were near at hand: the American Academy of Political and Social Science (AAPSS) of Philadelphia, and the Academy of

Political Science of Columbia University (APS), both of which comprised leading corporate liberal businessmen, financiers, and corporate attorneys, as well as academics. Each of these organizations, along with the American Association for the Advancement of Science (AAAS), held symposia on monetary affairs during the winter of 1907–1908, and each called for the establishment of a central bank. The Columbia conference was organized by the distinguished Columbia economist E. R. A. Seligman, who not coincidentally was a member of the family of the prominent Wall Street investment bank of J. & W. Seligman and Company. Seligman was grateful that the university was able to provide a platform for leading bankers and financial journalists to promote a central bank, especially because "it is proverbially difficult in a democracy to secure a hearing for the conclusions of experts." Emphasizing the importance of a central bank at the meetings, in addition to Seligman, was National City Bank's Frank Vanderlip, Morgan's Chase National Bank's A. Barton Hepburn, and Kuhn, Loeb's Paul M. Warburg.

At the American Academy of Political and Social Science symposium in Philadelphia, several leading investment bankers as well as Comptroller of the Currency William B. Ridgely came out for a central bank. Members of the AAPSS's advisory committee on currency included Hepburn; Morgan personal attorney and statesman Elihu Root; Morgan's long-time personal attorney Francis Lynde Stetson; and J. P. Morgan himself. In the meanwhile, the AAAS symposium in January, 1908 was organized by none other than Charles A. Conant himself, who happened to be chairman of the AASS's social and economic section that year. Speakers favoring a central bank included Conant, Columbia economist J. B. Clark, Vanderlip, and Vanderlip's friend George E. Roberts, head of the Rockefeller-oriented Commercial National Bank of Chicago, who would later wind up at the National City Bank.

The task of the bank reformers was well summarized by J. R. Duffield, secretary of the Bankers Publishing Company, in January 1908: "It is recognized generally that before legislation can be had there must be an educational campaign carried on, first among the bankers, and later among commercial organizations, and finally among the people as a whole."

During the same month, the legislative lead in banking reform was taken by Senator Nelson W. Aldrich (R., R.I.), head of the Senate Finance Committee, and, as the father-in-law of John D. Rockefeller, Jr., Rockefeller's man in the U. S. Senate. Aldrich's Aldrich-Vreeland Act passed Congress that year, its most prominent provision the increased amount of emergency currency that national banks could issue. A more important if widely neglected provision, however, established a National Monetary Commission (NMC) that would investigate the currency question and suggest proposals for comprehensive banking reform. The underlying purpose of the NMC was revealed by two admirers who hailed this new proposal. Seren S. Pratt of the *Wall Street Journal* conceded that the real purpose of the NMC was to swamp the public with supposed expertise, thereby "educating" them into accepting banking reform. Pratt pointed out that "in no other way can such education be effected more thoroughly and rapidly than by . . . a commission." Another function of a commission, noted Festus J. Wade, a St. Louis banker and member of the Currency Commission of the American Bankers Association, was to "keep the financial issue out of politics," and put it squarely in the safe custody of carefully selected "experts." The Indianapolis Monetary Commission was now being recreated on a national scale.

Senator Aldrich lost no time in launching the NMC, in June 1908. The Commission consisted of an equal number of Senators and Representatives, but these members of Congress were mere window-dressing to the advisors and staff who did the real work of the Commission. From the beginning, Aldrich envisioned the NMC, and the banking reform movement generally, to be run as an alliance of Rockefeller, Morgan, and Kuhn, Loeb people. Aldrich chose as the leading experts advising or joining the Commission two men suggested by Morgan leaders. As his top adviser, Aldrich chose, on the suggestion of J. P. Morgan, seconded by Jacob Schiff, probably the most powerful of the Morgan partners, Henry P. Davison. For leading technical economic expert and director of research, Aldrich accepted the recommendation of Roosevelt's close friend and fellow Morgan man, Harvard University President Charles Eliot, who had urged the appointment of Harvard economist Abram Piatt Andrew. Andrew commissioned and supervised numerous reports and studies on all relevant aspects of banking and finance. In December, Aldrich hired the inevitable Charles A. Conant for research, public relations, and agitprop for the NMC. Meanwhile, Aldrich gathered around him inner circles of influential advisers, who included Warburg and Vanderlip. Warburg gathered around him subcircles who included

Irving T. Bush, head of the Currency Committee of the New York Merchants Association, and men from the top ranks of the American Economic Association, to which Warburg delivered an address advocating central banking in December, 1908. Warburg met and corresponded frequently with leading academic economists who favored banking reform, including Seligman; Davis R. Dewey, historian of banking at M.I.T., long-time secretary-treasurer of the American Economic Association and brother of the progressive philosopher and educator John Dewey; Frank W. Taussig; Irving Fisher of Yale; and Oliver M. W. Sprague, Professor of Banking at Harvard, of the Morgan-oriented Sprague family.

In the month of September, 1909, the reformers accelerated their drive for a central bank into high gear. Morgan-oriented Chicago banker George M. Reynolds delivered a presidential address to the American Bankers Association flatly calling for a central bank for America. Almost simultaneously on September 14, President William Howard Taft, speaking in Boston, suggested that the country seriously consider a central bank. Taft had been close to the reformers, especially to his Rockefeller-oriented friend Nelson Aldrich, since 1900. The *Wall Street Journal* understood the importance of this public address, as "removing the subject from the realm of theory to that of practical politics."

One week later, the bank reformers organized a virtual government-bank-media complex to drive through a central bank. On September 22, the *Wall Street Journal* began an unprecedented front-page, fourteen-part series of editorials entitled "A Central Bank of Issue." These unsigned editorials were actually written by the ubiquitous Charles A. Conant, from his vantage point as salaried chief propagandist of the U. S. government's National Monetary Commission. Building on his experience in 1898, Conant, aided by Aldrich's secretary, prepared abstracts of commission materials and distributed them to newspapers in early 1910. J. P. Gavitt, head of the Washington bureau of the Associated Press, was recruited by the NMC to extract "newsy paragraphs" for newspaper editors out of commission abstracts, articles, and forthcoming books. And two ostensibly disinterested academic organizations lent their coloration to the NMC: the Academy of Political Science, publishing a special volume of its *Proceedings* in collaboration with the NMC, "to popularize, in the best sense, some of the valuable work of the Commission." In the meanwhile, the Academy of Political and Social Science published its own special volume in 1910, *Banking Problems*, introduced by Andrew, and including articles by veteran bank reformers, including Johnson, Horace White, and Morgan Bankers Trust official Fred I. Kent, as well as by a number of high officials of Rockefeller's National City Bank of New York.

Meanwhile, Paul M. Warburg capped his lengthy and intensive campaign for a central bank in a famous speech to the New York YMCA on March 23, 1910, on "A United Reserve Bank for the United States." Warburg outlined the structure of his beloved German *Reichsbank*, but he was careful to allay the fears of Wall Street by insisting that the central bank would not be "controlled by 'Wall Street' or any monopolistic interest." Therefore, Warburg insisted that the new Reserve Bank must not be *called* a "central bank," and that the Reserve Bank's governing board be chosen by government officials, merchants and bankers; bankers, of course, were to dominant the selections.

One of the great cheerleaders for the Warburg Plan, and the man who introduced the volume on banking reform featuring Warburg's speech and published by the Academy of Political Science (H. R. Mussey, ed., *The Reform of the Currency*, New York, 1911), was kinsman and Seligman investment banking family economist, E. R. A. Seligman. So delighted, too, with Warburg's speech was the Merchants' Association of New York that it distributed thirty thousand copies of the speech during the spring of 1910. Warburg had carefully paved the way for this action by the Merchants' Association by regularly meeting with the Currency Committee of the Merchants Association since the fall of 1908. Warburg's efforts were aided by the fact that the resident expert for that committee was Joseph French Johnson.

During the same spring of 1910, the NMC's numerous research volumes on various aspects of banking poured forth onto the market. The object was to swamp public opinion with a parade of impressive analytic and historical scholarship, all allegedly "scientific" and "value-free," but all designed to further the agenda of a central bank.

Culmination at Jekyll Island

Now that the groundwork had been laid for a central bank among scholars, bankers, and interested public opinion, by the latter half of 1910 it was time to formulate a concrete practical plan and to focus the rest of the agitation to push it through. As Warburg wrote in the Academy of Political Science book on

Reform of the Currency: "Advance is possible only by outlining a tangible plan" to set the terms of the debate.

The tangible plan phase of the central bank movement was launched by the ever-pliant Academy of Political Science of Columbia University, which held a monetary conference in November, 1910, in conjunction with the New York Chamber of Commerce and the Merchants' Association of New York. The members of the NMC were the joint guests of honor at this conclave, and delegates to it were chosen by governors of twenty-two states, as well as presidents of twenty-four chambers of commerce. Also attending this conference were a large number of economists, monetary analysts and representatives of the nation's leading bankers. Attendants at the conference included Frank Vanderlip, Elihu Root, Jacob Schiff, Thomas W. Lamont, partner of the Morgan bank, and J. P. Morgan himself. The formal sessions of the conference were organized around papers delivered by Laughlin, Johnson, Bush, Warburg, and Conant. C. Stuart Patterson, Dean of the University of Pennsylvania Law School and member of the finance committee of the Morgan-oriented Pennsylvania Railroad, who had been the chairman of the first IMC and a member of the Indianapolis Monetary Commission, laid down the marching orders for the assembled troops. He recalled the great lesson of the IMC, and the way its proposals had triumphed because "we went home and organized an aggressive and active movement." He then exhorted the troops: "That is just what you must do in this case, you must uphold the hands of Senator Aldrich. You have got to see that the bill which he formulates . . . obtains the support of every part of this country."

With the movement fully primed, it was now time for Senator Aldrich to write the bill. Or rather, it was time for the senator, surrounded by a few of the topmost leaders of the financial elite, to go off in seclusion, and hammer out a detailed plan around which all parts of the central banking movement could rally. Someone, probably Henry P. Davison, got the idea of convening a small group of top leaders in a super-secret conclave, to draft the bill. The eager J. P. Morgan arranged for a plush private conference at his exclusive millionaire's retreat, at the Jekyll Island Club on Jekyll Island, Georgia. Morgan was a co-owner of the club. On November 22, 1910, Senator Aldrich, with a handful of companions, set forth under assumed names in a privately chartered railroad car from Hoboken, New Jersey to the coast of Georgia, allegedly on a duck-hunting expedition.

The conferees worked for a solid week at the plush Jekyll Island retreat, and hammered out the draft of the bill for the Federal Reserve System. Only six people attended this super-secret week-long meeting, and these six neatly reflected the power structure within the bankers' alliance of the central banking movement. The conferees were, in addition to Aldrich (Rockefeller kinsman); Henry P. Davison, Morgan partner; Paul Warburg, Kuhn Loeb partner; Frank A. Vanderlip, vice-president of Rockefeller's National City Bank of New York; Charles D. Norton, president of Morgan's First National Bank of New York; and Professor A. Piatt Andrew, head of the NMC research staff, who had recently been made an Assistant Secretary of the Treasury under Taft, and who was a technician with a foot in both the Rockefeller and Morgan camps.

The conferees forged the Aldrich Bill, which, with only minor variations, was to become the Federal Reserve Act of 1913. The only substantial disagreement at Jekyll Island was tactical: Aldrich attempted to hold out for a straightforward central bank on the European model, while Warburg, backed by the other bankers, insisted that political realities required the reality of central control to be cloaked in the palatable camouflage of "decentralization." Warburg's more realistic, duplicitous tactic won the day.

Aldrich presented the Jekyll Island draft, with only minor revisions, to the full NMC as the Aldrich Bill in January, 1911. Why then did it take until December, 1913 for Congress to pass the Federal Reserve Act? The hitch in the timing resulted from the Democratic capture of the House of Representatives in the 1910 elections, and from the looming probability that the Democrats would capture the White House in 1912. The reformers had to regroup, drop the highly partisan name of Aldrich from the bill, and recast it as a Democratic bill under Virginia's Representative Carter Glass. But despite the delay and numerous drafts, the structure of the Federal Reserve as passed overwhelmingly in December 1913 was virtually the same as the bill that emerged from the secret Jekyll Island meeting three years earlier. Successful agitation brought bankers, the business community, and the general public rather easily into line.

The top bankers were brought into camp at the outset; as early as February, 1911, Aldrich organized a closed-door conference of twenty-three leading bankers at Atlantic City. Not only did this conference of bankers endorse the Aldrich Plan, but it was made clear to them that "the real purpose of the conference was to discuss winning the banking community over to government control directly by the bankers for their own ends." The big bankers at the conference also realized that the Aldrich Plan would "increase the power of the big national banks to compete with the rapidly growing state banks, (and) help bring the state banks under control."[33]

By November, 1911, it was easy to line up the full American Bankers Association behind the Aldrich Plan. The threat of small bank insurgency was over, and the nation's banking community was now lined up solidly behind the drive for a central bank. Finally, after much backing and filling, after Aldrich's name was removed from the bill and Aldrich himself decided not to run for reelection in 1912, the Federal Reserve Act was passed overwhelmingly on December 22, 1913, to go into effect in November of the following year. As A. Barton Hepburn exulted to the annual meeting of the American Bankers Association in late August 1913: "The measure recognizes and adopts the principles of a central bank. Indeed, if it works out as the sponsors of the law hope, it will make all incorporated banks together joint owners of a central dominating power."[34]

The Fed At Last:
Morgan-Controlled Inflation

The new Federal Reserve System had finally brought a central bank to America: the push of the big bankers had at last

---

[33]Kolko, *Triumph of Conservatism*, p. 186.
[34]Ibid., p. 235.

succeeded. Following the crucial plank of post-Peel Act Central Banking, the Fed was given a monopoly of the issue of all bank notes; national banks, as well as state banks, could now only issue deposits, and the deposits had to be redeemable in Federal Reserve Notes as well as, at least nominally, in gold. All national banks were "forced" to become members of the Federal Reserve System, a "coercion" they had long eagerly sought, which meant that national bank reserves had to be kept in the form of demand deposits, or checking accounts, at the Fed. The Fed was now in place as lender of last resort; and with the prestige, power, and resources of the U. S. Treasury solidly behind it, it could inflate more consistently than the Wall Street banks under the National Banking System, and above all, it could and did, inflate even during recessions, in order to bail out the banks. The Fed could now try to keep the economy from recessions that liquidated the unsound investments of the inflationary boom, and it could try to keep the inflation going indefinitely.

At this point, there was no need for even national banks to hold onto gold; they could, and did, deposit their gold into the vaults of the Fed, and receive reserves upon which they could pyramid and expand the supply of money and credit in a coordinated, nation-wide fashion. Moreover, with reserves now centralized into the vaults of the Fed, bank reserves could be, as the bank apologists proclaimed, "economized," i.e., there could be and was more inflationary credit, more bank "counterfeiting," pyramided on top of the given gold reserves. There were now three inverted inflationary pyramids of bank credit in the American economy: the

Fed pyramided *its* notes and deposits on top of its newly centralized gold supply; the national banks pyramided bank deposits on top of their reserves of deposits at the Fed; and those state banks who chose not to exercise their option of joining the Federal Reserve System could keep their deposit accounts at national banks and pyramid *their* credit on top of that. And at the base of the pyramid, the Fed could coordinate and control the inflation by determining the amount of reserves in the member banks.

To give an extra fillip to monetary inflation, the new Federal Reserve System cut in half the average legal minimum reserve requirements imposed on the old national banks. Whereas the national banks before the onset of the Fed were required to keep an average minimum of 20 percent reserves to demand deposits, on which they could therefore pyramid inflationary money and credit of 5:1, the new Fed halved the minimum reserve requirement on the banks to 10 percent, doubling the inflationary bank pyramiding in the country to 10:1.

As luck would have it, the new Federal Reserve System coincided with the outbreak of World War I in Europe, and it is generally agreed that it was only the new system that permitted the U.S. to enter the war and to finance both its own war effort, and massive loans to the allies; roughly, the Fed doubled the money supply of the U.S. during the war and prices doubled in consequence. For those who believe that U.S. entry into World War I was one of the most disastrous events for the U.S. and for Europe in the twentieth century, the facilitating of U.S. entry into the war is scarcely a major point in favor of the Federal Reserve.

In form as well as in content, the Federal Reserve System is precisely the cozy government-big bank partnership, the government-enforced banking cartel, that big bankers had long envisioned. Many critics of the Fed like to harp on the fact that the private bankers legally own the Federal Reserve System, but this is an unimportant legalistic fact; Fed (and therefore possible bank) profits from its operations are taxed away by the Treasury. The benefits to the bankers from the Fed come not from its legal profits but from the very essence of its operations: its task of coordination and backing for bank credit inflation. *These* benefits dwarf any possible direct profits from the Fed's banking operations into insignificance.

From the beginning, the Fed has been headed by a Federal Reserve Board in Washington, all appointed by the President with the consent of the Senate. The Board supervises the twelve "decentralized" regional Federal Reserve Banks, whose officers are indeed selected by private banks in each region, officers who have to be approved by the Washington Board.

At the outset of the Fed, and until the "reforms" of the 1930s, the major control of the Fed was not in the hands of the Board, but of the Governor (now called "President") of the Federal Reserve Bank of New York, Wall Street's main man in the Fed System.[35] The major instrument of Fed

[35]Because of the peculiarities of banking history, "Governor" is considered a far more exalted title than "President," a status stemming from the august title of "Governor" as head of the original and most prestigious Central Bank, the Bank of England. Part of the downgrading of the regional Federal Reserve Banks and upgrading of power of the Washington Board in the 1930s was reflected in the change of the title of head of each regional Bank from "Governor" to "President," matched by the change of title of the Washington board from "Federal Reserve Board" to "Board of Governors of the Federal Reserve System."

control of the money and banking system is its "open market operations": its buying and selling of U.S. government securities (or, indeed, any other asset it wished) on the open market. (We will see how this process works below.) Since the U.S. bond market is located in Wall Street, the Governor of the New York Fed was originally in almost sole control of the Fed's open market purchases and sales, and hence of the Federal Reserve itself. Since the 1930s, however, the crucial open market policies of the Fed have been decided by a Federal Open Market Committee, which meets in Washington, and which includes all the seven members of the Board of Governors plus a rotating five of the twelve largely banker-selected Presidents of the regional Feds.

There are two critical steps in the establishment and functioning of any cartel-like government regulation. We cannot afford to ignore either step. Step one is passing the bill and establishing the structure. The second step is selecting the proper personnel to run the structure: there is no point to big bankers setting up a cartel, for example, and then see the personnel fall into the "wrong" hands. And yet conventional historians, not geared to power elite or ruling elite analysis, usually fall down on this crucial second task, of seeing precisely *who* the new rulers of the system would be.

It is all too clear, on examining the origin and early years of the Fed, that, both in its personnel and chosen monetary and financial policies, the Morgan Empire was in almost supreme control of the Fed.

This Morgan dominance was not wholly reflected in the makeup of the first Federal Reserve Board. Of the seven Board members, at the time two members were automatically and *ex officio* the Secretary of the Treasury and the Comptroller of the Currency, the regulator of the national banks who is an official in the Treasury Department. The Secretary of Treasury in the Wilson Administration was his son-in-law William Gibbs McAdoo, who, as a failing businessman and railroad magnate in New York City, had been personally befriended and bailed out by J. P. Morgan and his close associates. McAdoo spent the rest of his financial and political life in the Morgan ambit. The Comptroller of the Currency was a long-time associate of McAdoo's, John Skelton Williams. Williams was a Virginia banker, who had been a director of McAdoo's Morgan controlled Hudson & Manhattan Railroad and president of the Morgan-oriented Seaboard Airline Railway.

These Treasury officials on the Board were reliable Morgan men, but they were members only *ex officio*. Governor (now "Chairman") of the original board was Charles S. Hamlin, whom McAdoo had appointed as Assistant Secretary of Treasury along with Williams. Hamlin was a Boston attorney who had married into the wealthy Pruyn family of Albany, a family long connected with the Morgan-dominated New York Central Railroad. Another member of the Federal Reserve Board, and a man who succeeded Hamlin as Governor, was William P. G. Harding, a protégé of Alabama Senator Oscar W. Underwood, whose father-in-law, Joseph H. Woodward, was vice-president of Harding's First National Bank of Birmingham, Alabama, and head of the Woodward Iron Company, whose board included representatives of both Morgan and Rockefeller interests. The other three Board members were Paul M. Warburg; Frederic A. Delano, uncle of Franklin D. Roosevelt and president of the Rockefeller-controlled Wabash Railway; and Berkeley economics professor Adolph C. Miller, who had married into the wealthy, Morgan-connected Sprague family of Chicago.[36]

Thus, if we ignore the two Morgan *ex-officios*, the Federal Reserve Board in Washington began its existence with one reliable Morgan man, two Rockefeller associates (Delano and a leader of close Rockefeller ally, Kuhn, Loeb), and two men of uncertain affiliation: a prominent Alabama banker, and an economist with vague family connections to Morgan interests. While the makeup of the Board more or less mirrored the financial power-structure that had been present at the Fed's critical founding meeting at Jekyll Island, it could scarcely guarantee unswerving Morgan control of the nation's banking system.

That control was guaranteed, instead, by the identity of the man who was selected to the critical post of Governor of the New York Fed, a man, furthermore, who was by temperament very well equipped to seize in fact the power that the structure of the Fed could offer him. That man, who ruled the Federal Reserve System with an iron hand

[36]Miller's father-in-law, Otho S. A. Sprague, had served as a director of the Morgan-dominated Pullman Company, while Otho's brother Albert A. Sprague, was a director of the Chicago Telephone Company, a subsidiary of the mighty Morgan-controlled monopoly American Telephone & Telegraph Company.

It should be noted that while the Oyster Bay-Manhattan branch of the Roosevelt family (including President Theodore Roosevelt) had long been in the Morgan ambit, the Hyde Park branch (which of course included F.D.R.) was long affiliated with their wealthy and influential Hudson Valley neighbors, the Astors and the Harrimans.

from its inception until his death in 1928, was one Benjamin Strong.[37]

Benjamin Strong's entire life had been a virtual preparation for his assumption of power at the Federal Reserve. Strong was a long-time protégé of the immensely powerful Henry P. Davison, number two partner of the Morgan Bank just under J. P. Morgan himself, and effective operating head of the Morgan World Empire. Strong was a neighbor of Davison's in the then posh suburb of New York, Englewood, New Jersey, where his three closest friends in the world became, in addition to Davison, two other Morgan partners; Dwight Morrow and Davison's main protégé as Morgan partner, Thomas W. Lamont. When the Morgans created the Bankers Trust Company in 1903 to compete in the rising new trust business, Davison named Strong as its secretary, and by 1914 Strong had married the firm's president's daughter and himself risen to president of Bankers Trust. In addition, the Davisons raised Strong's children for a time after the death of Strong's first wife; moreover, Strong served J. P. Morgan as his personal auditor during the Panic of 1907.

Strong had long been a voluble advocate of the original Aldrich Plan, and had participated in a lengthy August, 1911 meeting on the Plan with the Senator Davison, Vanderlip and a few other bankers on Aldrich's yacht. But Strong was bitterly disappointed at the final structure of the Fed, since he wanted a "real central bank . . . run from New York by a

[37]On the personnel of the original Fed, see Murray N. Rothbard, "The Federal Reserve as a Cartelization Device: The Early Years, 1913–1939," in *Money in Crisis*, Barry Siegel, ed. (San Francisco: Pacific Institute for Public Policy Research, 1984), pp. 94–115.

board of directors on the ground"—that is, a Central Bank openly and candidly run from New York and dominated by Wall Street. After a weekend in the country, however, Davison and Warburg persuaded Strong to change his mind and accept the proffered appointment as Governor of the New York Fed. Presumably, Davison and Warburg convinced him that Strong, as effective head of the Fed, could achieve the Wall Street-run banking cartel of his dreams if not as candidly as he would have wished. As at Jekyll Island, Warburg persuaded his fellow cartelist to bow to the political realities and adopt the cloak of decentralization.

After Strong assumed the post of Governor of the New York Fed in October, 1914, he lost no time in seizing power over the Federal Reserve System. At the organizing meeting of the System, an extra-legal council of regional Fed governors was formed; at its first meeting, Strong grabbed control of the council, becoming both its chairman and the chairman of its executive committee. Even after W. P. G. Harding became Governor of the Federal Reserve Board two years later and dissolved the council, Strong continued as the dominant force in the Fed, by virtue of being named sole agent for the open-market operations of all the regional Federal Reserve Banks. Strong's power was further entrenched by U.S. entry into World War I. Before then, the Secretary of the Treasury had continued the legally mandated practice since Jacksonian times of depositing all government funds in its own sub-treasury branch vaults, and in making all disbursements from those branches. Under spur of wartime, however, McAdoo fulfilled Strong's long-standing ambition: becoming the sole fiscal agent for the U.S.

Treasury. From that point on, the Treasury deposited its funds with the Federal Reserve.

Not only that: wartime measures accelerated the permanent nationalizing of the gold stock of Americans, the centralization of gold into the hands of the Federal Reserve. This centralization had a twofold effect: it mobilized more bank reserves to spur greater and nationally-coordinated inflation of bank credit; and it weaned the average American from the habit of using gold in his daily life and got him used to substituting paper or checking accounts instead. In the first place, the Federal Reserve law was changed in 1917 to permit the Fed to issue Federal Reserve Notes in exchange for gold; before that, it could only exchange its notes for short-term commercial bills. And second, from September, 1917 until June, 1919 the United States was *de facto* off the gold standard, at least for gold redemption of dollars to foreigners. Gold exports were prohibited and foreign exchange transactions were controlled by the government. As a result of both measures, the gold reserves of the Federal Reserve, which had constituted 28 percent of the nation's gold stock on U.S. entry into the war, had tripled by the end of the war to 74 percent of the country's gold.[38]

The content of Benjamin Strong's monetary policies was what one might expect from someone from the highest strata

[38]On Benjamin Strong's seizure of supreme power in the Fed and its being aided by wartime measures, see Lawrence E. Clark, *Central Banking Under the Federal Reserve System* (New York: Macmillan, 1935), pp. 64–82, 102–5; Lester V. Chandler, *Benjamin Strong: Central Banker* (Washington, D.C.: Brookings Institution, 1958), pp. 23–41, 68–78, 105–7; and Henry Parker Willis, *The Theory and Practice of Central Banking* (New York: Harper & Brothers, 1936), pp. 90–91.

of Morgan power. As soon as war broke out in Europe, Henry P. Davison sailed to England, and was quickly able to use long-standing close Morgan ties with England to get the House of Morgan named as sole purchasing agent in the United States, for the duration of the war, for war material for Britain and France. Furthermore, the Morgans also became the sole underwriter for all the British and French bonds to be floated in the U.S. to pay for the immense imports of arms and other goods from the United States. J. P. Morgan and Company now had an enormous stake in the victory of Britain and France, and the Morgans played a major and perhaps decisive role in maneuvering the supposedly "neutral" United States into the war on the British side.[39]

The Morgan's ascendancy during World War I was matched by the relative decline of the Kuhn, Loebs. The Kuhn, Loebs, along with other prominent German-Jewish investment bankers on Wall Street, supported the German side in the war, and certainly opposed American intervention on the Anglo-French side. As a result, Paul Warburg was ousted from the Federal Reserve Board, the very institution he had done so much to create. And of all the leading "Anglo" financial interests, the Rockefellers, ally of the Kuhn, Loebs, and a bitter rival of the Angle-Dutch Royal Dutch Shell Oil Company for world oil markets and resources, was one of the very few who remained unenthusiastic about America's entry into the war.

---

[39]On the Morgans, their ties to the British, and their influence on America's entry into the war, see Charles Callan Tansill, *America Goes to War* (Boston: Little, Brown, 1938).

During World War I, Strong promptly used his dominance over the banking system to create a doubled money
supply so as to finance the U. S. war effort and to insure an
Anglo-French victory. All this was only prelude for a Mor-
gan-installed monetary and financial policy throughout the
1920s. During the decade of the twenties, Strong collaborated
closely with the Governor of the Bank of England, Montagu
Norman, to inflate American money and credit so as to
support the return of Britain to a leading role in a new form
of bowdlerized gold standard, with Britain and other European countries fixing their currencies at a highly over-valued
par in relation to the dollar or to gold. The result was a
chronic export depression in Britain and a tendency for
Britain to lose gold, a tendency that the United States felt
forced to combat by inflating dollars in order to stop the
hemorrhaging of gold from Great Britain to the U.S.

The New Deal and the
Displacement of the Morgans

It was not only through Benjamin Strong that the Morgans
totally dominated American politics and finance during the
1920s. President Calvin Coolidge, who succeeded Rockefeller ally President Harding when he died in office, was a close
personal friend of J. P. Morgan, Jr., and a political protégé of
Coolidge's Amherst College classmate, Morgan partner
Dwight Morrow, as well as of fellow Morgan partner
Thomas Cochran. And throughout the Republican administrations of the 1920s, the Secretary of the Treasury was mul-
timillionaire Pittsburgh tycoon Andrew W. Mellon, whose
Mellon interests were long-time allies of the Morgans. And

while President Herbert Hoover was not nearly as intimately connected to the Morgans as Coolidge, he had long been close to the Morgan interests. Ogden Mills, who replaced Mellon as Treasury Secretary in 1931 and was close to Hoover, was the son of a leader in such Morgan railroads as New York Central; in the meanwhile, Hoover chose as Secretary of State Henry L. Stimson, a prominent disciple and law partner of Morgan's one-time personal attorney, Elihu Root. More tellingly, two unofficial but powerful Hoover advisers during his administration were Morgan partners Thomas W. Lamont (the successor to Davison as Morgan Empire CEO) and Dwight Morrow, whom Hoover regularly consulted three time a week.

A crucial aspect of the first term of the Roosevelt New Deal, however, has been sadly neglected by conventional historians: The New Deal constituted a concerted Bringing Down and displacement of Morgan dominance, a coalition of opposition financial out-groups combined in the New Deal to topple it from power. This coalition was an alliance of the Rockefellers; a newly-burgeoning Harriman power in the Democratic Party; newer and brasher Wall Street Jewish investment banks such as Lehman Brothers and Goldman Sachs pushing Kuhn, Loeb into the shade; and such ethnic out-groups as Irish Catholic buccaneer Joseph P. Kennedy, Italian-Americans such as the Giannini family of California's Bank of America, and Mormons such as Marriner Eccles, head of a vast Utah banking-holding company-construction conglomerate, and allied to the California-based Bechtel Corporation in construction and to the Rockefeller's Standard Oil of California.

The main harbinger of this financial revolution was the Rockefeller's successful takeover of the Morgan's flagship commercial bank, the mighty Chase National Bank of New York. After the 1929 crash, Winthrop W. Aldrich, son of Senator Nelson Aldrich and brother-in-law of John D. Rockefeller, Jr., engineered a merger of his Rockefeller-controlled Equitable Trust Company into Chase Bank. From that point on, Aldrich engaged in a titanic struggle within Chase, by 1932 managing to oust the Morgan's Chase CEO Albert Wiggin and to replace him by Aldrich himself. Ever since, Chase has been the virtual general headquarters of the Rockefeller financial Empire.

The new coalition cunningly drove through the New Deal's Banking Acts of 1933 and 1935, which transformed the face of the Fed, and permanently shifted the crucial power in the Fed from Wall Street, Morgan, and the New York Fed, to the politicos in Washington, D.C. The result of these two Banking Acts was to strip the New York Fed of power to conduct open-market operations, and to place it squarely in the hands of the Federal Open Market Committee, dominated by the Board in Washington, but with regional private bankers playing a subsidiary partnership role.[40]

---

[40]See, in particular, Thomas Ferguson, "Industrial Conflict and the Coming of the New Deal: the Triumph of Multinational Liberalism in America," in *The Rise and Fall of the New Deal Order, 1930–1980*, Steve Fraser and Gary Gerstle, eds. (Princeton: Princeton University Press, 1989), pp. 3–31. Also see the longer article by Ferguson, "From Normalcy to New Deal: Industrial Structure, Party Competition, and American Public Policy in the Great Depression," *Industrial Organization* 38, no. 1 (Winter 1984).

The other major monetary change accomplished by the New Deal, of course, and done under cover of a depression "emergency" in the fractional reserve banking system, was to go off the gold standard. After 1933, Federal Reserve Notes and deposits were no longer redeemable in gold coins to Americans; and after 1971, the dollar was no longer redeemable in gold bullion to foreign governments and central banks. The gold of Americans was confiscated and exchanged for Federal Reserve Notes, which became legal tender; and Americans were stuck in a regime of fiat paper issued by the government and the Federal Reserve. Over the years, all early restraints on Fed activities or its issuing of credit have been lifted; indeed, since 1980, the Federal Reserve has enjoyed the absolute power to do literally *anything* it wants: to buy not only U.S. government securities but any asset whatever, and to buy as many assets and to inflate credit as much as it pleases. There are no restraints left on the Federal Reserve. The Fed is the master of all it surveys.

In surveying the changes wrought by the New Deal, however, we should refrain from crying for the Morgans. While permanently dethroned by the first term of the New Deal and never returned to power, the Morgans were able to take their place, though chastened, in the ruling New Deal coalition by the end of the 1930s. There, they played an important role in the drive by the power elite to enter World War II, particularly the war in Europe, once again on the side of Britain and France. During World War II, furthermore, the Morgans played a decisive behind-the-scenes role in hammering out the Bretton Woods Agreement with

Keynes and the British, an agreement which the U.S. government presented as a *fait accompli* to the assembled "free world" at Bretton Woods by the end of the war.[41]

Since World War II, indeed, the various financial interests have entered into a permanent realignment: the Morgans and the other financial groups have taken their place as compliant junior partners in a powerful "Eastern Establishment," led unchallenged by the Rockefellers. Since then, these groups, working in tandem, have contributed rulers to the Federal Reserve System. Thus, the present Fed Chairman, Alan Greenspan, was, before his accession to the throne a member of the executive committee of the Morgans' flagship commercial bank, Morgan Guaranty Trust Company. His widely revered predecessor as Fed Chairman, the charismatic Paul Volcker, was a long-time prominent servitor of the Rockefeller Empire, having been an economist for the Rockefellers' Exxon Corporation, and for their headquarters institution, the Chase Manhattan Bank. (In a symbolically important merger, Chase had absorbed Kuhn, Loeb's flagship commercial bank, the Bank of Manhattan.) It was indeed a New World, if not a particularly brave one; while there were still to be many challenges to Eastern Establishment financial and political power by brash newcomers and takeover buccaneers from Texas and California, the old-line Northeastern interests had themselves become harmoniously solidified under Rockefeller rule.

---

[41]See G. William Domhoff, *The Power Elite and the State: How Policy is Made in America* (New York: Aldine de Gruyter, 1990), pp. 113–41; 159–81.

Deposit "Insurance"

We have not yet examined another important change wrought in the U.S. financial system by the New Deal. In 1933, it proclaimed assurance against the rash of bank failures that had plagued the country during the Depression. By the advent of Franklin Roosevelt, the fractional-reserve banking system had collapsed, revealing its inherent insolvency; the time was ripe for a total and genuine reform, for a cleansing of the American monetary system by putting an end, at long last, to the mendacities and the seductive evils of fractional-reserve banking. Instead, the Roosevelt Administration unsurprisingly went in the opposite direction: plunging into massive fraud upon the American public by claiming to rescue the nation from unsound banking through the new Federal Deposit Insurance Corporation (FDIC). The FDIC, the Administration proclaimed, had now "insured" all bank depositors against losses, thereby propping up the banking system by a massive bailout guaranteed in advance. But, of course, it's all done with smoke and mirrors. For one thing, the FDIC only has in its assets a tiny fraction (1 or 2 percent) of the deposits it claims to "insure." The validity of such governmental "insurance" may be quickly gauged by noting the late 1980s catastrophe of the savings and loan industry. The deposits of *those* fractional-reserve banks had supposedly nestled securely in the "insurance" provided by another federal agency, the now-defunct, once-lauded Federal Savings and Loan Insurance Corporation.

One crucial problem of deposit "insurance" is the fraudulent application of the honorific term "insurance" to schemes such as deposit guarantees. Genuine insurance gained its benevolent connotations in the public mind from the fact that, when applied properly, it works very well. Insurance properly applies to risks of future calamity that are not readily subject to the control of the individual beneficiary, and where the incidence can be predicted accurately in advance. "Insurable risks" are those where we can predict an incidence of calamities in large numbers, but not in individual cases: that is, we know nothing of the individual case except that he or it is a member of a certain class. Thus, we may be able to predict accurately how many people aged 65 will die within the next year. In that case, individuals aged 65 can pool annual premiums, with the pool of premiums being granted as benefits to the survivors of the unlucky deceased.

The more, however, that may be known about the individual cases, the more these cases need to be segregated into separate classes. Thus, if men and women aged 65 have different average death rates, or those with different health conditions have varying death rates, they must be divided into separate classes. For if they are not, and say, the healthy and the diseased are forced into paying the same premiums in the name of egalitarianism, then what we have is no longer genuine life insurance but rather a coerced redistribution of income and wealth.

Similarly, to be "insurable" the calamity has to be outside the control of the individual beneficiary; otherwise, we encounter the fatal flaw of "moral hazard," which again takes the plan out of genuine insurance. Thus, if there is fire insurance in a certain city, based on the average incidence of fire in different kinds of buildings, but the insured are allowed to set the fires to collect the insurance without discovery or penalty, then again genuine insurance has given way to a redistributive racket. Similarly, in medicine, specific diseases such as appendicitis may be predictable in large classes and therefore genuinely insurable, but simply going to the doctor for a checkup or for vague ills is not insurable, since this action is totally under the control of the insured, and therefore cannot be predicted by insurance firms.

There are many reasons why business firms on the market can in no way be "insured," and why the very concept applied to a firm is absurd and fraudulent. The very essence of the "risks" or uncertainty faced by the business entrepreneur is the precise opposite of the measurable risk that can be alleviated by insurance. Insurable risks, such as death, fire (if not set by the insured), accident, or appendicitis, are homogeneous, replicable, random, events that can therefore be grouped into homogeneous classes which can be predicted in large numbers. But actions and events on the market, while often similar, are inherently unique, heterogeneous, and are not random but influencing each other, and are therefore inherently uninsurable and not subject to grouping into homogeneous classes measurable in advance. Every event in human action on the market is unique and unmeasurable. The entrepreneur is precisely the person who faces and bears the inherently *un*insurable risks of the marketplace.[42]

---

[42]This crucial difference was precisely the most important insight of the classic work by Frank H. Knight, *Risk, Uncertainty and Profit*, 3rd ed. (London: London School of Economics, [1921] 1940).

But if no business firm can ever be "insured," how much more is this true of a fractional-reserve bank! For the very essence of fractional-reserve banking is that the bank is inherently insolvent, and that its insolvency will be revealed as soon as the deluded public realizes what is going on, and insists on repossessing the money which it mistakenly thinks is being safeguarded in its trusted neighborhood bank. If no business firm can be insured, then an industry consisting of hundreds of insolvent firms is surely the last institution about which anyone can mention "insurance" with a straight face. "Deposit insurance" is simply a fraudulent racket, and a cruel one at that, since it may plunder the life savings and the money stock of the entire public.

How the Fed Rules and Inflates

Having examined the nature of fractional reserve and of central banking, and having seen how the questionable blessings of Central Banking were fastened upon America, it is time to see precisely how the Fed, as presently constituted, carries out its systemic inflation and its control of the American monetary system.

Pursuant to its essence as a post-Peel Act Central Bank, the Federal Reserve enjoys a monopoly of the issue of all bank notes. The U. S. Treasury, which issued paper money as Greenbacks during the Civil War, continued to issue one-dollar "Silver Certificates" redeemable in silver bullion or coin at the Treasury until August 16, 1968. The Treasury has now abandoned any note issue, leaving all the country's paper notes, or "cash," to be emitted by the Federal Reserve. Not only that; since the U.S. abandonment of the gold standard in 1933, Federal Reserve Notes have been legal tender for all monetary debts, public or private.

Federal Reserve Notes, the legal monopoly of cash or "standard," money, now serves as the base of two inverted pyramids determining the supply of money in the country. More precisely, the assets of the Federal Reserve Banks consist largely of two central items. One is the gold originally confiscated from the public and later amassed by the Fed. Interestingly enough, while Fed liabilities are no longer redeemable in gold, the Fed safeguards its gold by depositing it in the Treasury, which issues "gold certificates" guaranteed to be backed by no less than 100 percent in gold bullion buried in Fort Knox and other Treasury depositories. It is surely fitting that the only honest warehousing left in the monetary system is between two different agencies of the federal government: the Fed makes sure that *its* receipts at the Treasury are backed 100 percent in the Treasury vaults, whereas the Fed does not accord any of *its* creditors that high privilege.

The other major asset possessed by the Fed is the total of U.S. government securities it has purchased and amassed over the decades. On the liability side, there are also two major figures: Demand deposits held by the commercial banks, which constitute the reserves of those banks; and Federal Reserve Notes, cash emitted by the Fed. The Fed is in the rare and enviable position of having its liabilities in the form of Federal Reserve Notes constitute the legal tender of the country. In short, its liabilities—Federal Reserve Notes— *are* standard money. Moreover, its other form of liability— demand deposits—are redeemable by deposit-holders (i.e., banks, who constitute the depositors, or "customers," of the

Fed) in these Notes, which, of course, the Fed can print at will. Unlike the days of the gold standard, it is impossible for the Federal Reserve to go bankrupt; it holds the legal monopoly of counterfeiting (of creating money out of thin air) in the entire country.

The American banking system now comprises two sets of inverted pyramids, the commercial banks pyramiding loans and deposits on top of the base of reserves, which are mainly their demand deposits at the Federal Reserve. The Federal Reserve itself determines its own liabilities very simply: by buying or selling assets, which in turn increases or decreases bank reserves by the same amount.

At the base of the Fed pyramid, and therefore of the bank system's creation of "money" in the sense of deposits, is the Fed's power to print legal tender money. But the Fed tries its best not to print cash but rather to "print" or create demand deposits, checking deposits, out of thin air, since *its* demand deposits constitute the reserves on top of which the commercial banks can pyramid a multiple creation of bank deposits, or "checkbook money."

Let us see how this process typically works. Suppose that the "money multiplier"—the multiple that commercial banks can pyramid on top of reserves, is 10:1. That multiple is the inverse of the Fed's legally imposed minimum reserve requirement on different types of banks, a minimum which now approximates 10 percent. Almost always, if banks *can* expand 10:1 on top of their reserves, they will do so, since that is how they make their money. The counterfeiter, after all, will strongly tend to counterfeit as much as he can legally get away with. Suppose that the Fed decides it wishes to expand the nation's total money supply by $10 billion. If the money multiplier is 10, then the Fed will choose to purchase $1 billion of assets, generally U.S. government securities, on the open market.

Figure 10 and 11 below demonstrates this process, which occurs in two steps. In the first step, the Fed directs its Open Market Agent in New York City to purchase $1 billion of U.S. government bonds. To purchase those securities, the Fed writes out a check for $1 billion on itself, the Federal Reserve Bank of New York. It then transfers that check to a government bond dealer, say Goldman, Sachs, in exchange

---

Figure 10
Fed Buys a $1 Billion Bond: Immediate Result

Commercial Banks

Assets	Equity + Liabilities
	Demand deposits (to Goldman, Sachs): + $1 billion.
Deposits at Fed (Reserves): + $1 billion	

The Federal Reserve

Assets	Equity + Liabilities
U.S. Government Securities: + $1 billion	Demand deposits to banks (Chase): + $1 billion

for $1 billion of U.S. government bonds. Goldman, Sachs goes to its commercial bank—say Chase Manhattan—deposits the check on the Fed, and in exchange increases its demand deposits at the Chase by $1 billion.

Where did the Fed get the money to pay for the bonds? It created the money out of thin air, by simply writing out a check on itself. Neat trick if you can get away with it!

Chase Manhattan, delighted to get a check on the Fed, rushes down to the Fed's New York branch and deposits it in its account, increasing its reserves by $1 billion. Figure 10 shows what has happened at the end of this Step One.

The nation's total money supply at any one time is the total standard money (Federal Reserve Notes) plus deposits in the hands of the public. Note that the *immediate* result of the Fed's purchase of a $1 billion government bond in the open market is to increase the nation's total money supply by $1 billion.

But this is only the first, immediate step. Because we live under a system of fractional-reserve banking, other consequences quickly ensue. There are now $1 billion more in reserves in the banking system, and as a result, the banking system expands its money and credit, the expansion beginning with Chase and quickly spreading out to other banks in the financial system. In a brief period of time, about a couple of weeks, the entire banking system will have expanded credit and the money supply another $9 billion, up to an increased money stock of $10 billion. Hence, the leveraged, or "multiple," effect of changes in bank reserves, and of the Fed's purchases or sales of assets which determine those reserves. Figure 11, then, shows the consequences of the Fed purchase of $1 billion of government bonds after a few weeks.

Note that the Federal Reserve balance sheet after a few weeks is unchanged in the aggregate (even though the specific banks owning the bank deposits will change as individual banks expand credit, and reserves shift to other banks who then join in the common expansion.) The change in totals has taken place among the commercial banks, who

---

Figure 11

Fed Buys a $1 Billion Bond:
Result After a Few Weeks

Commercial Banks

Assets	Equity + Liabilities
Loans and securities: + $9 billion	Demand deposits: + $10 billion
Deposits at Fed (Reserves): + $1 billion	

The Federal Reserve

Assets	Equity + Liabilities
U.S. Government Securities: + $1 billion	Demand deposits to banks: +$1 billion

---

have pyramided credits and deposits on top of their initial burst of reserves, to increase the nation's total money supply by $10 billion.

It should be easy to see why the Fed pays for its assets with a check on itself rather than by printing Federal Reserve Notes. Only by using checks can it expand the money supply by ten-fold; it is the Fed's demand deposits that serve as the base of the pyramiding by the commercial banks. The power to print money, on the other hand, is the essential base in which the Fed pledges to redeem its deposits. The Fed only issues paper money (Federal Reserve Notes) if the public demands cash for its bank accounts and the commercial banks then have to go to the Fed to draw down their deposits. The Fed wants people to use checks rather than cash as far as possible, so that it can generate bank credit inflation at a pace that it can control.

If the Fed purchases any asset, therefore, it will increase the nation's money supply immediately by that amount; and, in a few weeks, by whatever multiple of that amount the banks are allowed to pyramid on top of their new reserves. If it *sells* any asset (again, generally U.S. government bonds), the sale will have the symmetrically reverse effect. At first, the nation's money supply will decrease by the precise amount of the sale of bonds; and in a few weeks, it will decline by a multiple, say ten times, that amount.

Thus, the major control instrument that the Fed exercises over the banks is "open market operations," purchases or sale of assets, generally U.S. government bonds. Another powerful control instrument is the changing of legal reserve minima. If the banks have to keep no less than 10 percent of their deposits in the form of reserves, and then the Fed suddenly lowers that ratio to 5 percent, the nation's money supply, that is of bank deposits, will suddenly and very rapidly double. And vice versa if the minimum ratio were suddenly raised to 20 percent; the nation's money supply will be quickly cut in half. Ever since the Fed, after having expanded bank reserves in the 1930s, panicked at the inflationary potential and doubled the minimum reserve requirements to 20 percent in 1938, sending the economy into a tailspin of credit liquidation, the Fed has been very cautious about the *degree* of its changes in bank reserve requirements. The Fed, ever since that period, has changed bank reserve requirements fairly often, but in very small steps, by fractions of one percent. It should come as no surprise that the trend of the Fed's change has been downward: ever lowering bank reserve requirements, and thereby increasing the multiples of bank credit inflation. Thus, before 1980, the average minimum reserve requirement was about 14 percent, then it was lowered to 10 percent and less, and the Fed now has the power to lower it to zero if it so wishes.

Thus, the Fed has the well-nigh absolute power to determine the money supply if it so wishes.[43] Over the years, the thrust of its operations has been consistently inflationary. For not only has the trend of its reserve requirements on the

---

[43]Traditionally, money and banking textbooks list three forms of Fed control over the reserves, and hence the credit, of the commercial banks: in addition to reserve requirements and open market operations, there is the Fed's "discount" rate, interest rate charged on its loans to the banks. Always of far more symbolic than substantive importance, this control instrument has become trivial, now that banks almost never borrow from the Fed. Instead, they borrow reserves from each other in the overnight "federal funds" market.

banks been getting ever lower, but the amount of its amassed U.S. government bonds has consistently increased over the years, thereby imparting a continuing inflationary impetus to the economic system. Thus, the Federal Reserve, beginning with zero government bonds, had acquired about $400 million worth by 1921, and $2.4 billion by 1934. By the end of 1981 the Federal Reserve had amassed no less than $140 billion of U.S. government securities; by the middle of 1992, the total had reached $280 billion. There is no clearer portrayal of the inflationary impetus that the Federal Reserve has consistently given, and continues to give, to our economy.

What Can Be Done?

It should by now be all too clear that we cannot rely upon Alan Greenspan, or any Federal Reserve Chairman, to wage the good fight against the chronic inflation that has wrecked our savings, distorted our currency, levied hidden redistribution of income and wealth, and brought us devastating booms and busts. Despite the Establishment propaganda, Greenspan, the Fed, and the private commercial bankers are not the "inflation hawks" they like to label themselves. The Fed and the banks are not part of the solution to inflation; they are instead part of the problem. In fact, they *are* the problem. The American economy has suffered from chronic inflation, and from destructive booms and busts, because that inflation has been invariably generated by the Fed itself. That role, in fact, is the very purpose of its existence: to cartelize the private commercial banks, and to help them inflate money and credit together, pumping in reserves to the banks, and bailing them out if they get into trouble. When the Fed was imposed upon the public by the cartel of big banks and their hired economists, they told us that the Fed was needed to provide needed stability to the economic system. After the Fed was founded, during the 1920s, the Establishment economists and bankers proclaimed that the American economy was now in a marvelous New Era, an era in which the Fed, employing its modern scientific tools, would stabilize the monetary system and eliminate any future business cycles. The result: it is undeniable that, ever since the Fed was visited upon us in 1914, our inflations have been more intense, and our depressions far deeper, than ever before.

There is only one way to eliminate chronic inflation, as well as the booms and busts brought by that system of inflationary credit: and that is to eliminate the counterfeiting that constitutes and creates that inflation. And the only way to do *that* is to abolish legalized counterfeiting: that is, to abolish the Federal Reserve System, and return to the gold standard, to a monetary system where a market-produced metal, such as gold, serves as the standard money, and not paper tickets printed by the Federal Reserve.

While there is no space here to go into the intricate details of how this could be done, its essential features are clear and simple. It would be easy to return to gold and to abolish the Federal Reserve, and to do so at one stroke. All we need is the will. The Federal Reserve is officially a "corporation," and the way to abolish it is the way any corporation, certainly any inherently insolvent corporation such as the Fed, is abolished. Any corporation is eliminated by liquidating its assets and parcelling them out *pro rata* to the corporation's creditors.

Figure 12 presents a simplified portrayal of the assets of the Federal Reserve, as of April 6, 1994.

Of the Federal Reserve assets, except gold, all are easily liquidated. The $345 billion of U.S. government and other federal government agency securities owned by the Fed should be simply and immediately canceled. This act would immediately reduce the taxpayers' liability for the public debt by $345 billion. And indeed, why in the world should taxpayers be taxed by the U.S. Treasury in order to pay interest and principal on bonds held by another arm of the federal government—the Federal Reserve? The taxpayers have to be sweated and looted, merely to preserve the accounting fiction that the Fed is a corporation independent of the federal government.

"Other Fed Assets," whether they be loans to banks, or buildings owned by the Fed, can be scrapped as well, although perhaps some of the assets can be salvaged. Treasury currency,

---

Figure 12
Federal Reserve Assets, April 6, 1994

$ in billions

Gold.......................................	11
U. S. Government and other Federal Securities...	345
Treasury Currency Outstanding + SDRs.........	30
Other Fed Assets...........................	35
Total.......................................	$421

---

simply old paper money issued by the Treasury, should quickly be canceled as well; and SDR's ($8 billion) were a hopeless experiment in world governmental paper that Keynesians had thought would form the basis of a new world fiat paper money. These two should be immediately canceled.

We are left with the $11 billion of the Fed's only real asset—its gold stock—that is supposed to back approximately $421 billion in Fed liabilities. Of the total Fed liabilities, approximately $11 billion is "capital," which should be written off and written down with liquidation, and $6 billion are Treasury deposits with the Fed that should be canceled. That leaves the Federal Reserve with $11 billion of gold stock to set off against $404 billion in Fed liabilities.

Fortunately for our proposed liquidation process, the "$11 billion" Fed's valuation of its gold stock is wildly phony, since it is based on the totally arbitrary "price" of gold at $42.22 an ounce. The Federal Reserve owns a stock of 260 million ounces of gold. How is it to be valued?

The gold stock of the Fed should be revalued upward so that the gold can pay off all the Fed's liabilities—largely Federal Reserve Notes and Federal Reserve deposits, at 100 cents to the dollar. This means that the gold stock should be revalued such that 260 million gold ounces will be able to pay off $404 billion in Fed liabilities.

When the United States was on the gold standard before 1933, the gold stock was fixed by definition at $20 per gold ounce; the value was fixed at $35 an ounce from 1933 until the end of any vestige of a gold standard in 1971. Since 1971 we have been on a totally fiat money, but the gold stock of the Fed has been arbitrarily valued by U.S. statutes at $42.22 an ounce. This has been an absurd undervaluation on its face, considering that the gold price on the world market has been varying from $350 to $380 an ounce in recent years. At any rate, as we return to the gold standard, the new gold valuation can be whatever is necessary to allow the Fed's stock of gold to be allocated 100 percent to all its creditors. There is nothing sacred about any initial definition of the gold dollar, so long as we stick to it once we are on the gold standard.

If we wish to revalue gold so that the 260 million gold ounces can pay off $404 billion in Fed liabilities, then the new fixed value of gold should be set at $404 billion divided by 260 million ounces, or $1555 per gold ounce. If we revalue the Fed gold stock at the "price" of $1555 per ounce, then its 260 million ounces will be worth $404 billion. Or, to put it another way, the "dollar" would then be *defined* as 1/1555 of an ounce.

Once this revaluation takes place, the Fed could and should be liquidated, and its gold stock parcelled out; the Federal Reserve Notes could be called in and exchanged for gold coins minted by the Treasury. In the meanwhile, the banks' demand deposits at the Fed would be exchanged for gold bullion, which would then be located in the vaults of the banks, with the banks' deposits redeemable to its depositors in gold coin. In short, at one stroke, the Federal Reserve would be abolished, and the United States and its banks would then be back on the gold standard, with "dollars" redeemable in gold coin at $1555 an ounce. Every bank would then stand, once again as before the Civil War, on its own bottom.

One great advantage of this plan is its simplicity, as well as the minimal change in banking and the money supply that it would require. Even though the Fed would be abolished and the gold coin standard restored, there would, at this point, be no outlawry of fractional-reserve banking. The banks would therefore be left intact, but, with the Federal Reserve and its junior partner, federal deposit insurance, abolished, the banks would, at last, be on their own, each bank responsible for its own actions.[44] There would be no lender of last resort, no taxpayer bailout. On the contrary, at the first sign of balking at redemption of any of its deposits in gold, any bank would be forced to close its doors immediately and liquidate its assets on behalf of its depositors. A gold-coin standard, coupled with instant liquidation for any bank that fails to meet its contractual obligations, would bring about a free banking system so "hard" and sound, that any problem of inflationary credit or counterfeiting would be minimal. It is perhaps a "second-best" solution to the ideal

---

[44]Some champions of the free market advocate "privatizing" deposit insurance instead of abolishing it. As we have seen above, however, fractional-reserve bank deposits are in no sense "insurable." How does one "insure" an inherently insolvent industry? Indeed, it is no accident that the first collapse of Saving and Loan deposit insurance schemes in the mid-1980s took place in the *privately*-run systems of Ohio and Maryland. Privatizing governmental functions, while generally an admirable idea, can become an unreflective and absurd fetish, if the alternative of *abolition* is neglected. Some government activities, in short, shouldn't exist at all. Take, for example, the government "function," prevalent in the old Soviet Union, of putting dissenters into slave labor camps. Presumably we would want such an activity not privatized, and thereby made more efficient, but eliminated altogether.

of treating fractional-reserve bankers as embezzlers, but it would suffice at least as an excellent solution for the time being, that is, until people are ready to press on to full 100 percent banking.

Index

Academy of Political Science (APS), 108, 113, 115

Aldrich, Nelson W., 110–111, 112, 115, 116, 117, 125, 130–131

Allison, William Boyd, 99

American Academy of Political and Social Science (AAPSS), 108–109, 113

American Association for the Advancement of Science (AAAS), 109

American Bankers Association, 105, 110–111, 112, 118

American Economics Association, 112

Andrew, Abram Piatt, 111, 116

Ann Arbor Business Men's Association, 100

Associated Press, 113

Atchison, Topeka, and Santa Fe Railroads, 100

Atlas Engine Works of Indianapolis, 94

Austrian School, 25–26

Bacon, Robert, 95

Bank Acts, 75

Bank of Amsterdam, 44, 54n

Bank of England, 58–59, 61ff, 121n

Bank of Manhattan, 133

Bank of North America, 72

bank runs, purpose of, 46, 50

Bankers, 9, 70, 71, 86, 117, 145

Bankers Trust Company, 125,

banking, accounting and, 31–33; as legitimate business, 31–33, 41, 57; as cartel, 53, 70, 122; competition in, 53–54, 84; criminal law and, 40ff; deposit banking, 33–40, 62; embezzlement, 35, 39, 40ff; fractional reserve, 29–33, 37ff, 40ff, 43ff, 47ff, 144, 149n; fraud (see embezzlement); insolvency, 45ff, 146; loan, 29–33; money-warehouse, 34ff, 37ff, 43

barter, 13–15

Bechtel Corp., 130

Bretton Woods Agreement, 132–133

Bryan, William Jennings, 82, 91, 93

Burch, Philip H. Jr., 92n

Bush, Irving T., 111, 115

business cycle, 40, 54–55, 119, 145

Cambridge Merchant's Association, 100

Cantillon, Richard, 25–26

Carr v. *Carr*, 42

Central Banking (see also Federal Reserve), 11, 12; origins of, 58–62; functions of, 58ff, 65ff; lender of last resort, 62ff, 70, 79, 108, 119; politics of, 71–72; Wall Street and, 79–80

Central Intelligence Agency, 3

Chandler, Lester V., 127n

Murray N. Rothbard (1926–1995) was the S.J. Hall distinguished professor of economics at the University of Nevada, Las Vegas, and dean of the Austrian School of economics. He served as vice president for academic affairs at the Ludwig von Mises Institute, was editor of the *Review of Austrian Economics*, and his writings appeared in many journals and publications.

Professor Rothbard received his B.S., M.A., and Ph.D. from Columbia University, where he studied under Joseph Dorfman. For more than ten years, he also attended Ludwig von Mises's seminar at New York University.

Professor Rothbard is the author of thousands of articles, and his 17 books include: *A History of Money and Banking in the United States*; *The Panic of 1819*; *Man, Economy, and State*; *Power and Market*; *America's Great Depression*; *The Mystery of Banking*; *For a New Liberty*; *The Ethics of Liberty*; the four-volume *Conceived in Liberty*; the two-volume *Logic of Action*; and the two-volume *An Austrian Perspective on the History of Economic Thought*.